OFFICESPEAK

OFFICESPEAK

THE WIN-WIN GUIDE TO TOUCHING BASE, GETTING THE BALL ROLLING, AND THINKING INSIDE THE BOX

BY D. W. MARTIN

SIMON SPOTLIGHT ENTERTAINMENT
New York   London   Toronto   Sydney

This book is intended to provide a humorous look at a topic of daily importance to all nine-to-fivers: namely, the corporate drivel known as "officespeak." It should be obvious to anyone who picks up this book that any references to historical events, real people, real entities, or real locales are used fictitiously and solely for comic effect. I'm glad I got that off my chest. Now that we're all on the same page, let's get down to business.

SSE

SIMON SPOTLIGHT ENTERTAINMENT
An imprint of Simon & Schuster
1230 Avenue of the Americas, New York, New York 10020
Text copyright © 2005 by David Martin
All rights reserved, including the right of reproduction in whole or in part in any form.
SIMON SPOTLIGHT ENTERTAINMENT and related logo are trademarks of Simon & Schuster, Inc.
Designed by Yaffa Jaskoll
The text of this book was set in Helvetica.
Manufactured in the United States of America
First Edition 10 9 8 7 6 5 4 3 2 1
Library of Congress Cataloging-in-Publication Data
Martin, D. W.
Officespeak : the win-win guide to touching base, getting the ball rolling, and thinking inside the box / by D. W. Martin.—1st ed.
p. cm.
ISBN 1-4169-0028-4 (alk. paper)
1. Work—Humor. I. Title.
PN6231.W644
818'.607—dc22
2004022978

TO J. L. MARTIN

ACKNOWLEDGMENTS

First and foremost, myself. You did it, D. W., and what a fine job you did. Am I impressed? You betcha. Not only are you a tremendous writer, you are also exceptionally handsome. No reason to be coy about that.

My family, in particular my mom, dad, brother, and grandmother. Thanks for raising me and thank you for your unconditional support. And for paying the detox bills.

I need to thank Owen Burke for recommending me for this project. You are a mensch. Thank you. And also PCR and the UCB Theater for providing a home away from home. Now I'm going to cry.

To everyone at Simon Spotlight Entertainment for their unbridled support and enthusiasm, in particular Rick Richter, Jennifer Bergstrom, and my editor, Tricia Boczkowski. Tricia's faith in this book defied my expectations. Thank you for all that you have done. And thanks to Emily Westlake for promptly sending the checks. My kneecaps are intact because of you.

I also want to thank Andrew Howley, Laura Tisdel, Ann Day, and Jennifer Huwer for reading the manuscript in its raw, incipient stages. Your comments were invaluable. However, any cumbersome phrases or unfunny sections are entirely their fault.

And finally, I need to thank my wife and best friend, Jynne, for her tireless support, humor, and patience. You are the best spitballing partner in the business. None of this is possible without you. Now, where's my beer?

TABLE OF CONTENTS

Beware of all enterprises that require new clothes.
—HENRY DAVID THOREAU

Greed is all right. . . . Greed is healthy. You can be greedy and still feel good about yourself.
—IVAN BOESKY

Let's Get the Excellence Edge
—HUMAN RESOURCES POSTER

INTER

Cross out previous address. Use

INTRODUCTION,

OR WHY YOU SHOULD LISTEN TO ME

Hello. If you've picked up this book, it probably means you've come to your senses and are considering working in an office rather than pursuing your dream of taking your scratch-off lottery winnings to surf the Australian Gold Coast or becoming a full-time flu-study guinea pig. Because let's face it—dreams are nice, but they don't pay the bills. When was the last time you saw a pony-riding–princess–ballerina—veterinarian making the big bucks? Or a switch-hitting–astronaut—superspy raking in the dough? Answer: never. So put down the quilting needles, toss that Peace Corps application in the incinerator, strap on a shirt and tie, and start making money.

Then again, perhaps you are already well on your way to a life of PowerPoint presentations, computer freezes, and copier jams, not to mention a raging case of carpal tunnel syndrome. Now, before you get defensive and sulk off, understand that I'm not criticizing you. I just don't want to see you sucked into the whirlpool of office malaise that claims the lives of so many promising workers. We sacrifice the best eight hours of our day pinned like moths in the suffocating display case that we call the office. Some break free from these confines, but most of us perpetually bump our heads on the glass ceiling until we fall limply to the ground, our little moth wings vainly trying to muster one last flight, our moth mouths gasping for air, our dusty moth bodies fading into oblivion.

But, dammit, it doesn't have to be that way. Be the moth that breaks free to endlessly circle that big, bright lightbulb known as success. You can make it happen; you just need to step up to the plate. The key to slam-dunking your success is mastering the inane language of the office—all those pat, empty phrases that sound important but mean nothing and those seemingly innocuous euphemisms that actually foretell massive layoffs or no year-end bonuses. Phrases like "strategic decision," "Let's make this happen, people," "Are we having fun yet?" and "worker efficiency measures," to list just a few. This is the language of the powerful: safe, vague, migraine-inducingly dull. If you master this language, you can control the information and, ergo, control the office. You can make everyone miserable instead of being the miserable one.

The key to parlaying your career into a success is understanding how to use officespeak. I can teach you this language. I can turn you into one of those people who make you throw up in your mouth every time they say something like, "Time to knuckle down, team," or "The squeaky wheel always gets the grease." I can transform you from a moth into Mothra. Trading in your principles for capital never hurt anyone.

The last thing you should ever do is put this book down. If you could have every word of this text grafted onto your skin, by all means do so. You think I'm crazy, don't you? Well, here's something you don't know about me: I worked my way up the corporate ladder and became CEO by the age of twenty-four, earned my first billion on my twenty-eighth birthday, and became king of the country I founded when I was thirty-six and a half. If that's crazy, then tie me down, give me a lobotomy, and fit me for an adult diaper.

Look, I too was in your position: sitting behind a desk, moving one stack of papers from pile A to pile B, dealing with an unbearable boss, getting minor promotions to keep me inching slowly toward that dangling carrot of a significant raise, finding myself bogged down by the office machinery. My eyes glazed over every time another mindless memo about "team unity" or "strategies to manage workplace change and transition" crossed my desk. I wanted to jump out the window whenever an interminable boardroom meeting became even more interminable because some gung-ho manager decided to rally the troops for the big end-of-quarter push. All the officespeak was draining the life out of me. I thought of quitting, following an old dream I had of establishing a soup kitchen in downtown Philadelphia, maybe helping those whom life had overlooked.

But just before I packed it all in and became a failure, I had a vision. J. P. Morgan came to me in a dream, wearing nothing but a feather boa and a thong (look, it was a dream, and I'd drunk a lot of tequila that night), and after a limber striptease, he coyly whispered, "I'm in room 254." The point is, I realized that I loved business; I loved the thought of making money. There are plenty of people who can dish out soup to homeless folk, but there is only one me. So for the next month, I collected every stray memo I could find, read through every corporate newsletter, sat in all the meetings, hung out at the watercooler for hours on end, watched hour after hour of corporate videos, and spent two whole days at a urinal making small talk. It was quite an education. I absorbed it all and turned the language that was once my enemy into a valuable tool. All those words and phrases such as "troubleshoot," "See me," and "Be my quarterback on this one, champ," no longer bothered or confused me. I appropriated them and caused a paradigm shift (don't worry, this will all be explained later).

Listen, my life now is great. I have a wife, two kids, and three mistresses. When the view from my penthouse in Paris bores me, I build a better Eiffel Tower. When I crave adventure, I kidnap some men, abandon them on my private island, and hunt them for sport. Envy away.

I want you to have that life too. And it's quite simple. By reading this book, you will learn how to master the byzantine language that is office-speak. I imagine that if your eyes have scrolled down this far, you can at least read. Congratulations! Reading is a diminishing art. (Of course, if you had as much money as I do, you could just hire someone to read this book for you. I once employed a man to read James Joyce's *Ulysses* for me, and after six months of furrowed brow he proclaimed it quite good. I now have him working his way through the John Grisham oeuvre.)

But I digress. Time is money, and the whole point of life is to take money from other people and keep it for yourself. To give you an example, this evening I have a very well-paid speaking gig at the Wharton School of the University of Pennsylvania, where I will deliver a lecture entitled "A Win-Win Proposition: Interfacing Synergy in a Go-To Environment." Now, if you are honest with yourself, this tongue twister probably makes very little sense to you (though by the end of this book, I guarantee you will be composing your own little riddles). All I know is that it sounds impressive, and for 100 percent of these businesspeople, that alone will suffice. That's right, 100 percent. I'll let you in on a little secret: Businesspeople are sheep. Dirty, cud-chewing sheep. If you know how to control these sheep, then, my friend, you will prosper. And how do you control them? Quite simply, through language—the language of the office.

Is officespeak nonsense? Of course it is. Wonderful, delightful nonsense that you can manipulate for your own benefit. Those unwieldy legal disclaimers at the end of e-mails? Throw in a few subliminal messages and watch as you rapidly ascend the corporate ladder. I did! Do you have an important presentation tomorrow for which you have nothing prepared? No worries. This book includes my surefire phrases for success, the same phrases I used when I convinced a local government to raze an orphanage to make way for the deluxe apartments I wanted to build, not to mention the time I bought Ecuador.

As you've probably guessed by now, I'm a bit of a maverick. I play by my own rules—I don't always drive on the right-hand side of the road, or tell my children I love them when they ask, or wash my hands after I use the bathroom. I've been known to embellish at times and to inflate my position by making up "true stories" about myself with prominent people. Despite such forays into fiction, in my heart I mean well. I'm still your best source on how to get ahead in life.

I wrote this book for people who prefer bossa nova to disco; for people who still care about circumventing SEC regulations; for people who, late at night, when all the world is asleep, think to themselves that maybe, just maybe, the British should recolonize parts of the world.

This book provides you with all the key words and phrases you need to know to impress your boss, wow your colleagues, and garner fame and fortune. Is this the Rosetta stone of officespeak? Yes. You can thank me later by sending donations, care of the publisher. Now excuse me as I slip into something a little more comfortable. We have work to do.

CHAPTER 1

HOW TO TALK LIKE A PROFESSIONAL

'm just going to come right out and say that this is the boring part of the book. The necessary but slightly tedious section before the fun starts. It's rather like the surgeon general's warning on a beer stating that you shouldn't operate heavy machinery while under the influence. You read it, think about it, and then do some joyriding on that wheat thresher. I do hope you appreciate how forthright I am being with you. I could have easily claimed that the next few pages would make for a more thrilling read than, say, free-falling 10,000 feet without a parachute. But I didn't. Because I want to gain your trust. Trust is the cornerstone of any business relationship, and I want us to be trust friends. I want you to trust everything I write.

This section deals with the technical aspects of officespeak, such as passive voice, circular reasoning, and rhetorical questions. These are the nuts and bolts of the Rube Goldberg contraption that is the language of the office. Obscurity, vagueness, and a noncommittal stance on everything define the essence of officespeak. No one wants to come out and say what they really think. It is much safer for the company and those up top to constantly cloak their language in order to hide how much they do know or, just as often, how much they don't know. And once you realize this, you can use their techniques to your advantage. I didn't get where I am today by putting my hand on the Bible and swearing to tell the truth; the truth is for the weak.

Yes, it's frustrating when you're on the receiving end of officespeak, but you'll work through it and your career will thank you. So let's dive in like the great Renaissance artists who dissected cadavers in order to better comprehend the human form. We'll immerse our hands in the abdominal cavity of officespeak—pushing aside the intestines, fingering our way past the gallbladder—and, God willing, we will emerge smarter and wiser for it.

Passive Voice

The bread and butter of press releases and official statements. For those who have forgotten their basic grammar, a sentence in the passive voice does not have an active verb. Thus, no one can take the blame for "doing" something, since nothing, grammatically speaking, has been done by anybody. Using the passive voice takes the emphasis off yourself (or the company). Here are a few examples of how the passive voice can render any situation guiltless:

  "Five hundred employees were laid off." (Not "The company laid off five hundred employees," or even worse, "I laid off five hundred employees." These layoffs occurred in a netherworld of displaced blame, in which the company and the individual are miraculously absent from the picture.)

- "A decision has been reached: You're fired."
- "The numbers were added wrong."
- "The papers were misplaced."
- "The Employee of the Month plaque was ripped off the wall."

The passive voice can be your best friend. Use it to get out of jams, deflect blame, and thwart responsibility. But there are times when you never want to use the passive voice, such as when you have good news to deliver:

- "Profits were increased by fifty percent using strategic marketing endeavors."

Never sell yourself short—take full credit, whether or not it's due. Let's make this baby active:

- "*I* increased profits by fifty percent using strategic marketing endeavors."

That's more like it.

Circular Reasoning

Another favorite when it comes time to deliver bad news. In circular reasoning, a problem is posited and a reason is given. Except that the reason is basically just a rewording of the problem. Pretty nifty. Here are some examples to better explain the examples:

- "Our profits are down because they did not go up."
- "People were laid off because there was a surplus of workers."
- "We didn't get the client because the client went to another firm."
- "I was late for work because I was not early."
- "I ate the last birthday doughnut because it was the last doughnut. Sorry."
- "I slept with the intern because she wanted to sleep with me."

You will encounter circular reasoning in the boardroom, at financial meetings, at any juncture when someone has screwed up or has to deliver bad news. It's a wonderful way to give a seemingly substantial answer so as to appear in control of the situation. In fact, that last excuse about the intern bought me three more years with my first wife. Don't be afraid to bring officespeak into the home.

Rhetorical Questions

The questions that ask for no answers. So why even ask the question? Because it makes it seem as though the listener is participating in a true dialogue. When your boss asks, "Who's staying late tonight?" you know he really means, "Anyone who wants to keep their job will work late." Still, there's that split second when you think you have a say in the matter, when you believe your opinion counts. Only to be reminded, yet again, that no one cares what you think. Are you ready for some examples?

☞ "Do you have a problem with the decisions I make?"
☞ "Everybody ready for the big fourth-quarter push?"
☞ "Who thinks it's okay not to try their hardest?"
☞ "Are we having fun yet?"
☞ "Who doesn't want to make a profit?"
☞ "Can I get a 'Let's go for it, team!'?"
☞ "Who wants to be known as a quitter?"
☞ "So you think you could do a better job than me?"

Rhetorical questions are most commonly found in human resources materials and during motivational speeches from management.

Hollow Statements

The second cousin of circular reasoning. Hollow statements make it seem as though something positive is happening (such as better profits or increased market share), but they lack any proof to support the claim.

☞ "Our company is performing better than it looks."

☞ "Once productivity increases, so will profits."

☞ "Most of our success derives from intangibles."

☞ "Outside of the numbers we're doing real good."

☞ "Even though we haven't shown a profit in over two years, we're just as successful as we've always been."

☞ "Money isn't everything."

☞ "Keep up the good work."

☞ "I love my job."

Hollow statements are a form of damage control, with an emphasis on putting a positive spin on a given situation. When uttered by a master, the hollow statement sounds like a substantial point; its emptiness slips unseen beneath the BS radar. These statements are great to use when you're being bombarded with questions after a big presentation, as they seem just like real answers. That's why, in my seminars, I refer to hollow statements as the "chameleon of office-speak." On my first kayak trip down the Amazon River I trapped a chameleon and even named him "Hollow Statements," out of deference to the aforementioned technique. Sadly, Hollow Statements never made it back to the United States; I had to eat him after my guide and our food supply were devoured by a school of piranhas. For six weeks, I survived on only bark, dirt, and my own filth as I waited for a rescue party. When they found me I weighed seventy pounds and bleated like a goat.

I Think, I Guess

Ever notice how few people in the business world say "I know"? Sure, you hear it occasionally, but more often, people say "I think" or "I guess" or "maybe" or "possibly." It is always best to leave yourself wiggle room whenever you make a proclamation. Never commit to anything. Whether it's a budget plan, a new hire, or a pitch to a client, remain as aggressively noncommittal as possible. Yes, of course you want to succeed, and that's the sentiment you will project. But if you throw in enough qualifying terms, then you will be able to say "I told you so" if everything fails. Hedge your bets, straddle the fence, play for both teams. You only put yourself in a corner when you say "I know." Be willing to sacrifice your smarts.

↗ "I think that's a great idea."

↗ "Yes, I think we can increase your revenues."

↗ "I guess he'll make a good VP."

↗ "I think we can make this a very successful campaign. Sure. Possibly most definitely."

↗ "We can bring your product to a new and diverse audience . . . maybe."

↗ "Quite possibly we can get those shipments out to you by tomorrow."

↗ "I guess we can maybe give you a raise. I think possibly sometime in the next three months."

Be sure to "think" and "guess" your way through your entire career. Sure, you'll tick off some people, but you'll never be the fall guy.

They and Them

Pronouns used to refer to the high-level management that no one has ever met, only heard whispers about. "They" are faceless and often nameless. And their decisions render those beneath them impotent to change anything. "They" fire people, "they" freeze wages, "they" make your life a living hell. It's not your boss who is responsible—he would love to reverse all these directives if he could. But you see, his hands are tied. "They" and "them" have more in common with the tooth fairy and "student athletes" than any CEO or chairman of the board. "They" don't exist. "They" are the bogeymen that allow your manager to proceed with unpopular moves and still save face. He can always blame "them" for the absence of a Christmas bonus or for his inability to promote you.

 "I'd love to give you that raise, you know I would. But they're the ones in charge."

 "Okay, gang, bad news, no more cargo shorts allowed. Hey, I love the casual look, but they hate it."

"They said we had to take away two vacation days this year. Unfair? Completely. Do I hate it? Of course I do. But it's what they want."

"This just in. They said you have to refer to me as the Messiah. A little strange, I know, but this came from up top. They must know what they're doing."

Remember, your goal is to one day be "them."

Obfuscation

A tendency to obscure, darken, or stupefy. The primary goal of the above techniques is, in the end, obfuscation. Whether it's by means of the methods outlined above or by injecting jargon-heavy phrases into sentences, corporations want to make their motives and actions as difficult to comprehend as possible. They hope to obscure the truth and camouflage their own lack of knowledge about the issue at hand. Good luck getting a straight answer from management when you have a question. They will resort to one of the above techniques to make it seem as though they are addressing your issue, when in reality they are either sidestepping it or giving you the runaround. (Remember those last two phrases—you'll be using them a lot when complaining to your colleagues.) A manager's speech looks like the bottom of the muddy Mississippi; it's as clear as a blind dog's cataract. At least that's what Ted Turner used to tell me.

Most of these examples should be familiar to you, since you probably encounter them every day at your workplace. Still, it's good to name and identify the various techniques so you'll know how to use them to your advantage the next time you're in a bind, screw up a project, or miss a deadline. With a little practice, you'll be crossing eyes in no time.

CHAPTER 2

THE HISTORY OF OFFICESPEAK

Since the dawn of time, organisms have possessed an instinctive desire to form committees, pore over pie charts, organize company softball games, and dole out layoffs. In fact, Charles Darwin originally entitled his theory of evolution "The Great Species Layoff: Becoming Expendable in the Animal Kingdom." Although in this case, "layoff" meant "extinction." Makes you feel a tad small complaining about your severance package now, doesn't it? Unlike the misinformed creature that decided it could do without lungs and thus doomed an entire species, you will not extinguish mankind because you fail to land the big account. Point being, the culture of the office, the language of the office, has been in our DNA since that first amoeba crawled out of the primordial sea and proclaimed, "I'm pushing the envelope, people. This is the next big thing!" His joy was short-lived, though, as he felt the jaws of the second amoeba to crawl out of the sea snap around his single-cell body, thus instituting the first known hostile takeover. Hence the phrase, "big fish in a small pond."

What follows is by no means a comprehensive history of office-speak, merely a highlight reel. It is important to know where we come from in order to know where we are going. You will also impress your colleagues with your knowledge of officespeak etymology. Who doesn't want to know that the phrase "bury 'em alive" arose out of the mistaken belief that the best way to cure the plague was by burying the infected alive? Good times, people, good times. Rest assured, everything that follows has been extensively researched and exhaustively fact-checked. As always, you can trust me.

THE OFFICE LANGUAGE OF THE ANCIENT GREEKS

Democracy, philosophy, bushy back hair, and homoerotic art, like so many other pillars of Western civilization, were born in ancient Greece. So too was officespeak.

Fifth-century B.C. Athens bustled with genius: Plato, Euripides, Pericles all roamed the marbled halls of this resplendent city-state. Poetry flourished, architecture reached new heights, and government opened itself to the people; man was becoming civilized. The concept of a free-market economy also took root in the rocky soil of this inspired land and with it the initial blossoming of officespeak. A Greek merchant by the name of Phaedrus Circumferopolous is credited with uttering the first business cliché: "No need to reinvent the wheel." He had a practical purpose for espousing this, though, since he is also credited with actually inventing the wheel. Phaedrus possessed a keen business acumen and realized that the fewer improvements he would have to make to his product, the higher the profit margin for himself. If he could dupe everyone into believing that the wheel needed no improvements, then he could monopolize the wheel-producing business and pocket a bundle. For the past 2,500 years we've been Phaedrus's pawns, living under the false assumption that the wheel is fine as is. But it's not. Next year my company will release the Whool 3000: The Wheel for the Next Millennium. I can't disclose the nature of the new and improved wheel, but here's a teaser: Think rhombus.

The cubicle also traces its lineage back to Athens. The brainchild of Todd Cubiculmachis, the cubicle's original purpose was as a prison cell for lepers, murderers, pedophiles, and the unambitious. The word "cubicle" in Greek means "place of despair and loneliness." After the Greeks decided that remote islands served as better asylums, Todd found himself with a slew of empty, unused cubicles. But what or who could fill them? It was only when he took a walk along the beach of the Aegean Sea that he realized his cubicle's true purpose. He spied a young man, a scribe, pausing from his work on the sun-dappled beach, blinding in its white brilliancy, to relax and take a break from his task while he ruminated upon the natural beauty that surrounded him. Todd blanched at the unproductivity of this young man and realized that workers needed an environment devoid of outside temptations in order to focus on their tasks. The cubicle proved the perfect location. Once the domain of the sick and the degenerate, it would now house a new prisoner: the worker. Although it cannot be verified, it is believed that the first cubicle featured an ill-shapen basketball hoop placed above the trash can as well as a pornographic fresco of Venus de Milo.

The Greeks gave us not just Plato's *Dialogues,* but even more importantly, the dialogue of business. Empty phrases and, at times, outright lies (see Phaedrus Circumferopolous) took the place of meaningful discussion that might actually solve problems instead of exacerbating them. And thus began man's descent into the officespeak doldrums.

Here are some prominent phrases whose roots can easily be traced back to ancient Greece:

- "Let's not reinvent the wheel."
- "That idea is as solid as a rock."
- "It's all Greek to me." (Ironically enough, the original connotation of this phrase was that the speaker understood entirely what was going on since, of course, they were all Greek.)
- "The Parthenon wasn't built in seven days."
- "Don't beat a dead slave."
- "The proof of the ambrosia is in the eating."
- "The whole nine orgiums."

HOW JESUS USHERED IN THE
ERA OF CASUAL FRIDAYS

Up through Jesus's time, businesses enforced a severe dress code. No sandals, no facial hair, and no loose-hanging garments. Togas had to be firmly secured around the waist and all men had to have their hair closely shorn. The Romans instituted these rules so they could look dashing and virile when later portrayed in Hollywood by the likes of Laurence Olivier, Marlon Brando, Richard Burton, and Joaquin Phoenix. But one young man, an intern at an accounting firm in Nazareth, took issue with these strictures. That young man was Larry, half brother to Jesus. Although not a follower of Jesus, he did admire how Jesus slept in late, wore whatever was lying around, and refused to shave or cut his hair. Tired of the draconian dress code and trying to show solidarity with his half brother, Larry went wild one Friday and wore a loose-hanging tunic, a pair of Birkenstocks, and a "What Would Jesus Do?" bracelet to work. His bosses were not amused. They crucified Larry after lunch. But his dream for a casual work environment lives on today. You can see it in the halter tops and tube tops, the frayed jean shorts and BrewThru T-shirts of today's workers. Yes, Larry, your slow and exceedingly painful death was worth it. So the next time you find yourself in a fashion dilemma, just ask: What Would Larry Do?

The following phrases came into fashion around 33 A.D.:

↝ "Let's throw Barry to the lions."

↝ "That new assistant thinks he walks on water."

↝ "The die has been cast, we have to deliver."

↝ "I'd hire his firm—they can turn water into wine."

↝ "Kate, you're such a miracle worker."

↝ "He definitely has his disciples."

"If we don't have a strategy in place for our meeting with the Roman governor, we're gonna get crucified."

THE DARK AGES OF OFFICE LIFE: CALLING IN PLAGUE

There's a reason historians refer to the Dark Ages as the "Dark Ages." It was a miserable time for everyone involved. If people weren't lancing boils or plucking hairs from warts, they sat in some corner muttering to themselves as their gruel got cold and their donkey died of smallpox. No one was going on spring break to Daytona. It was just miserable all around.

Before the Middle Ages people had never called in sick. There was nothing to get sick about. Oh sure, maybe a cold here and there or a sprained ankle from throwing the javelin too hard, but on the whole life was good. Then the bubonic plague happened. No one knows for certain how this devastating disease began, but most experts agree: Journey's European tour of 1235 facilitated its rapid spread.

Everyone started to die horrible, excruciating deaths. It was difficult to work when you had puss oozing from every orifice. So companies decided to allocate ten sick days per calendar year to each employee. It was one of the few generous gestures in corporate history, yet barely anyone ever made it alive through their allotted days. Those who stayed healthy received "Mr. Punctual" awards, and if you showed up at work every day for two years, you received a pile of compost and spoiled goat milk. Again, just a bad time all around to be in the workforce.

But not all was lost. Out of the pain and suffering of the Dark Ages arose these classic phrases:

"Why don't we boil this down to the essentials?"

"We'll bury 'em alive."

"We have no choice but to bleed 'em."

"They have me working the graveyard shift." (During the Dark Ages this referred to normal operating business hours.)

"The proof of the blood pudding is in the eating" (a direct carry-over from the Greeks' ambrosia statement, but with a fun Dark Ages twist).

"The system is infected."

THE FIRST WHISTLE-BLOWER: SIR THOMAS MORE

Sir Thomas More serves as an example of how not to behave more than anything else. Yes, people laud him today for his integrity, but look what that integrity got him: beheaded. I've always lived by the maxim that it is better to go through life as a coward and a hypocrite than to die an early death just because you believed in some cause and tried to act nobly.

And I have to imagine that anyone who operates in the business world abides by that principle as well.

For those of you not as familiar with sixteenth-century English history, here is a quick primer on Sir Tom: When Henry VIII's first wife, Catherine of Aragon, failed to produce a male heir, Henry requested a divorce. The pope refused to grant one, so Henry did the only sensible thing a man in his position could do: He created the Church of England and placed himself at its head. And who among us hasn't thought of creating a new religion when things haven't gone our way?

More warned Henry against such a move. He said that he could not show fealty to the king as head of the Church of England. We won't go into More's reasons—there's a very dull movie starring Paul Scofield that can answer all of your questions—but suffice it to say the king, his boss, wasn't pleased. And back in the day, bosses possessed much greater control over the mortality of their employees. The king condemned More as a traitor and had him beheaded.

Sir Thomas committed the cardinal sin of openly questioning his employer. He went public, so to speak, and he paid the price. Remember: When in doubt, keep your mouth shut. It's not always going to be like Enron where you're feted and get to pose for *Playboy*. Sir Thomas More didn't have to make a big deal out of the whole oath of allegiance. He could have just quit and bummed around in France. But he possessed a nagging little monster known as a conscience. The moral here: Destroy your conscience.

We have Sir Thomas's executioner to thank for the following phrases:

- "Give them a heads-up."
- "We're gonna lose our heads on this one."
- "I can't make heads or tails of this."
- "Let's make a clean break."
- "Everyone's running around like they've just lost their heads."
- "I'm putting my neck on the line for you."
- "Heads are gonna roll!"

Then some stuff happened for a hundred years or so. The Spanish Inquisition gave us the infamous phrase "You're fired," as well as "Let's stretch this one out." But besides that, nothing of note happened until we arrive at the Enlightenment.

GOOD TIMES TO BAD TIMES: FROM THE ENLIGHTENMENT TO TODAY

The Enlightenment brought about the advent of the forty-hour work week, personal days, smoke breaks, interoffice romance, and vending machines. For a brief period of time work became civilized. People wore knee-length white breeches, satin coats, powdered wigs, and fake moles while being entertained by harpsichordists and early afternoon marionette shows during the week. Suddenly everyone wanted to work. All you had to do was look pretty and watch puppets whack each other with mallets. This wasn't the Dark Ages anymore! Work took on an aura of leisure, of fun. Who wouldn't want to make a quick buck seated at a loom, weaving a scene of lambs flitting about the meadow?

However, the joyride that was work during the Enlightenment had to come to an end. In the late eighteenth century factories and muscles were invented. This development proved most unfortunate for those entering the workforce imagining a life of blissful employment punctuated by tea breaks and poetry competitions to ascertain who could compose the most deliriously nonsensical limerick. Instead, these same would-be dilettantes and poets suffered under some of the harshest work conditions since the Dark Ages, when just making it to work alive was a victory. Their lives epitomized toil and hardship. It was the industrial revolution, and work truly began to suck.

But out of this proletarian pain blossomed these sayings:

- "I've invested a lot of sweat and blood in this project."
- "I don't want this to cost me an arm and a leg."
- "This backbreaking labor is gonna kill me."
- "The squeaky wheel always gets the grease."
- "I've been given a crushing workload."
- "You need to help me—I'm stuck. No, really, my arm is caught in the press."

Middle management really came to the fore during the industrial revolution and perfected the art of misinformation, most notably in the claims of one British coal mining company that coal dust doubled as a facial scrub. Most of your parents toiled in the industrial revolution and probably have the artificial limbs to show for it. Anyway, the industrial revolution ended on March 3, 1997, and gave way to the digital age, which we live in now. So enough with the past, let's get started with the present day.

CHAPTER 3

MY WEAKNESS IS THAT I'M A PERFECTIONIST: MASTERING THE ART OF THE INTERVIEW

"Interview" . . . the word itself, not unlike the word "colonoscopy," sends shivers up and down a person's spine. In other phases of your professional life, when nerves get the better of you, you can always blame someone else or cover your tracks. But in the interview, you can hide nothing.

The interview. Say it again. Let the word roll around on your tongue like a glass of 1936 Château Lafitte Rothschild. Do you taste the tannins? Now spit out the word. Yes, spit it out. Empower yourself. You own the word, you own the situation. Do not be afraid of the interview, never show the interview fear, for it will maul you like a wild boar on the veldt. The interview knows no mercy; it destroys at will. Just stay calm; don't think about all the hard work you've put into this fateful moment and how devastating it would be if you didn't get the job. Relax, it's only going to determine the rest of your life.

I've interviewed hundreds of people over the course of my career, and I've compiled personal dossiers on most of them. Some of those files I've sold to marketing companies in a clear breach of all privacy laws; others I've added to my personal collection for those gloomy days when I need a laugh. I know what trips people up; I know what you should say and what you shouldn't. The interviewer is not your friend; he wants you to fail. He wants to tell stories to his pals about "the retarded dude" he just interviewed. He wants to laugh at you. But if you follow a few simple guidelines, the interviewer won't be laughing—he'll be congratulating you on your new job.

STAY SOBER:
AND OTHER HELPFUL HINTS FOR
MAKING A GOOD FIRST IMPRESSION

It may seem obvious, but I can't tell you how many seemingly qualified candidates trip over this first hurdle. Show up drunk and you probably won't get the job. It's that simple.

Once you get past that, it should be fairly basic. Suit, tie, no sneakers, clean shaven, and for the ladies, classic black pumps, miniskirt, and a low-cut blouse—this ain't rocket science. However, you don't want to fall into anonymity, another freshly scrubbed recruit decked out in your Sunday best. Here are a few ways you can differentiate yourself from every other interviewee.

They say you never have a second chance to make a first impression. And until man builds a time machine, that statement will be true for a very long time. Your entrance is key. Enter like a lamb and you'll be thought of as a pushover, but enter like a lion and you'll earn immediate respect. As soon as you spot the secretary, toss your keys in her direction and tell her to park your car. "It's the one with the vanity plates: FUTURE CEO." Brash, ballsy, slightly misogynistic? Yes, yes, and yes. Impressive? Double yes. Your prospective employer loves to see a candidate who knows his place in the pecking order and feels comfortable exerting his superiority. People are in lower-paid positions for a reason: They're not as good as you.

Once you've established your authority and are firmly ensconced in the interviewer's office, you need to make an immediate impression. Light up a Cuban cigar, offer your interviewer one as well, make a joke about the "porous Canadian border," and then put your feet up on the desk. The interviewer needs to realize that he's not dealing with another schlub from the temp agency—he has a major player on his hands. Equip yourself with at least two cell phones and two beepers, and if you have the time, purchase an ankle holster for one of your phones—it's a nice touch. Prearrange for a friend to call your various phones and beepers at different times throughout the interview. This isn't being rude; this is being important. Apologize each time for the interruption and explain that these are emergency phone calls, that you are a team leader and must handle these matters immediately. "I guess I'm just too important," you can say by way of apology.

Let the interviewer overhear the following remarks and he'll realize that he's dealing with a true power broker:

 "If you had just listened to me the first time, this mess wouldn't have happened. Okay, calm down, don't worry, I'll fix this when I get back."

"That's great news! Just as I predicted, we turned around a fifteen percent profit. I told you my idea would work."

 "No, please, please, enough, you don't need to thank me anymore. I can't imagine I'm the best team leader you've ever worked with, but thanks for the compliment. You're too kind. No, you're more wonderful. Okay, fine, I'm more wonderful."

You can't spend the entire interview on the phone, though. There are some tricky questions that still need answering. But have no fear, you'll be more than prepared for the worst.

"Tell Me About Yourself."

When interviewers ask you to talk about yourself, what are they looking for? What does "yourself" really mean? Or even "about"? Or for that matter, "me"? But this is not the time for rumination, it's time for fabrication.

Interviewers want you to paint a picture for them of what you can bring to the company. Always use "I" statements; prospective employers want to know what *you* bring to the table—none of this "we" nonsense. Remember, there may be no "I" in team, but there sure as heck is one in "You're hired."

When talking about yourself, stress your accomplishments, even if you have to stretch the truth or just flat-out lie. Interviewers are looking for a couple of short anecdotes that display your leadership skills and your problem-solving abilities. The following story can be used to satisfy both requirements. Don't worry, nobody ever checks up on the validity of these kinds of tales.

> "There was a fire in the office. Raging. I'm the fire warden on our floor and I gathered all the employees into our safety area, handed out protective vests and glow sticks, and calmly led everyone to the fire exits. I then returned to my desk, got back on the phone, and closed a deal that made us a couple million dollars. When the firefighters finally showed up, I had managed to contain the fire to a small area with some copier toner and the watercooler. They made me an honorary firefighter. . . . Shucks, I told myself I wouldn't tell this story to anyone, makes it seem like I'm bragging."

"What's Your Biggest Weakness?"

This question is the darling of every interviewer and the proverbial ground ball through Bill Buckner's legs for those on the cusp of getting the job. How you answer this question determines whether you will live on Park Avenue or solicit donations outside the neighborhood OTB for the rest of your life. So, no pressure, but you have to hit this one out of the park.

When interviewers asks for your weaknesses, they are trying

to get a sense of how severely you will screw up the company. If you answer that your weakness is numbers, for instance, then you might cause the financial collapse of the company if you worked in the accounting department.

The first and most important thing to remember is: *Do not* tell the truth. You will only end up embarrassing yourself. I provide, as evidence, some of the most common weaknesses I've heard over the past twenty years:

- "My biggest weakness would definitely be my online gambling addiction."
- "Two words: crystal meth. Besides that, I'm golden."
- "Role-playing games. I love coming to work dressed as the white elf princess Saramunda."
- "Drooling. I have an acute drooling problem and have been known to short-circuit my keyboard."
- "Fluorescent lights."
- "An inability to take direction and to focus on the task at hand. Outside of that, I function perfectly in an office environment."
- "Beanie Babies!"
- "Kids are my big weakness. I just love picking kids off the street and taking them home with me."
- "My biggest weakness would have to be brownies. My second biggest weakness would probably be my bulimia."
- "I wet myself during times of crisis."

You can see how easy it would be to reveal your true, pathetic, vulnerable self. But how humiliating! Let these honest answers be a warning to you—many a qualified candidate has fallen into the weakness trap.

Below, I've listed four answers that any interviewer would love to hear:

- "My biggest weakness is my ability to make too much profit for the company."
- "My biggest weakness is my killer instinct. When I smell blood in the water, I attack like a shark feasting on a gaggle of drowning paraplegic kittens."
- "My biggest weakness would be that I'm an addict—addicted to efficiency and cost-saving measures. Every time I downsize employees, I feel like I'm on a cocaine high."
- "My biggest weakness would be the hard-on I get every time I underbid my competitor."

Now those are weaknesses any company could employ!

"Where Do You See Yourself in Five Years?"

One of the final questions of the job interview. I call it a "Goldilocks question," because the interviewer is looking for someone ambitious but not too ambitious, someone who is a hard worker but still has a life outside the office. This is one of the few times when you should show a softer side of your personality, let your prospective employer know that you're not just a ravenous, bloodthirsty profit monster. You have a heart as well. Make it past this classic query and you'll be able to smell that new corner office. Mmmmm, mahogany.

Good Answers

↝ "I hope to have earned my MBA on evenings and weekends so I can bring more knowledge and creativity to this company."

↝ "Getting a pat on the back from you, sir, for yet another week of outstanding hard work."

↝ "I hope in five years I'll have learned and achieved enough that I can be a mentor and inspiration to the more junior members of the department."

↝ "By then I hope to have mastered the day-to-day tasks well enough that I'll have time to tutor elementary school students once a week and still make it to practice for the company softball team."

Bad Answers

↝ "Sitting right where you are, waving to you in the parking lot as you carry out your box of family photos and personal possessions."

↝ "I don't know. I'm kind of a dreamer. Maybe teaching yoga somewhere, or being a parent, enjoying life and figuring out what it all means."

↝ "Possibly in jail. I ran over a drifter. I had been drinking, he was wearing earth-tone clothing, it was late, I never saw him. I think I washed all the blood, hair, and brain matter off my bumper, but you never know. There's no statute of limitations on murder . . . so long as no one finds out, I'll be right here."

✐ "Hopefully not a virgin anymore."

Follow these guidelines and you'll have no difficulty getting hired. It might even be too easy.

True Story: Golfing with Jack Welch

Jack Welch and I host an annual golf tournament held on my private resort in the South Pacific. On the fifth hole of last year's tourney (a nasty dogleg, par four), as we waited for the natives to squash the scorpions on the putting green, I asked Jack, "What's the secret of your success?" He smiled, winked, took the Cookie Monster bootie off his driver, and said, "Verbal acrobatics." He then nailed a 250-yard drive, middle of the green. Perfect. "And golf lessons." We both shared a good laugh over that one. Unfortunately, our approach shots to the green were delayed due to a careless native getting stung by a scorpion. All in all, though, it was a wonderful round of golf.

Now that you've landed the big job, you'll need to learn how to avoid the pitfalls of corporate propaganda. Pour yourself a tumbler of thirty-year-old Macallan and read on.

CHAPTER 4

THIS WON'T HURT ONE BIT: CORPORATE INOCULATION, AKA MOTIVATIONAL PROPAGANDA

A tyrannous organization thrives around you—two floors above you, down the hall, maybe even in the office next to yours. Like a vine it grows without notice until it has suffocated your soul. This organization thrives on doublespeak, false slogans, and manipulation. It rules with an iron fist, prying into every aspect of your life; it reads everything you write, it knows everything you see. Its absolute control over your every move would make Joseph Stalin blanch; it is beyond even the nightmarish vision of George Orwell. This group governs international banks, federal agencies, hospitals, and even day care centers. Its tentacles know no bounds. I speak, of course, of only one such organization: the Human Resources department.

Up through World War II the Nazis possessed one of the greatest propaganda machines in history. Posters, films, slogans, 401(k) programs, the Germans had it all. So it was only appropriate that as NASA stocked up on German rocket scientists after the war, so too did the Human Resources departments of major corporations pilfer the Nazi bureaucratic masterminds. The results: men on the moon and the first corporate softball picnic.

The Human Resources department is the most sophisticated distributor of misinformation since the Rutherford B. Hayes administration—

don't think we've forgotten you, Rutherford. Cross HR at your own peril. That I'm even writing this chapter and revealing their trade secrets has placed me in great jeopardy.

THE WELCOME VIDEO:
YOU WILL LIKE THIS COMPANY

Soaring images of your company's building, sweeping shots of America's purple mountains' majesty with the company logo branded on every scene, the inspiring chorus of Beethoven's Ninth Symphony cascading around you as you see montage after montage of all the wonderful things your company does for the world—this is the artistry of the corporate welcome video. This is the beginning of your corporate indoctrination.

"Hey there, new person, welcome to the company. I know you will have a marvelous time here. C'mon, let's meet some of the people who make this such a great place to work," the film's narrator intones in a soothing, narcotic lilt.

The welcome video makes the office seem like Walt Disney World on Paxil. Everyone smiling and waving as the camera passes by—they look like they couldn't be happier than when hunched over their desks crunching numbers and entering data. Yes, the workers seem to be saying, we love being drones, and so will you! This is the only time the office will resemble a happy, carefree environment.

The language of the video, like so much of the material Human

Resources distributes, is geared toward kindergartners. It is a soothing language, a reassuring language, a positive language. Phrases such as "the company will help you fulfill your potential," "the promise of a new day," and "exceeding yourself through work," permeate the narration like aphorisms from Mao's Little Red Book. You forget yourself for a moment and start to believe that the company can make you a better person. If you've ever belonged to a cult (and full disclosure here: I spent six weeks with David Koresh's Branch Davidians, never regretted a second), you are familiar with HR's tactics. They cultivate a familial bond with their employees, making them dependent on the company for their feelings of self-worth.

In your initial meeting, the HR folks will also emphasize how diverse the work environment is, as though the office is a zoo and they've stocked it full of exotic species. Look, there's a person in a wheelchair! And could that be a black man sitting at a computer? Why, yes, it is! Never mind that those might be the only two minorities in the office, they will be trotted out at every opportunity as beacons of the company's enlightened stance. Don't be shocked if, in the middle of your training, either one of these people makes a "surprise" visit.

This HR meeting is the first in a long line of corporate brainwashing techniques. Much like heroin, or pledging a fraternity or sorority, the corporation-as-family concept initially provides a soft, balmy feeling to the user or inductee. The sting of the needle gives way to the dreamlike sensation that you finally belong somewhere. And that's how the company gets you hooked. You become a junkie craving the corporation's love.

THIS COMPANY ROCKS!: IT'S ALL OVER THESE PENS, PENCILS, AND MOUSE PADS

HR's primary job is cultivating corporate pride among the workers. They ply you with tote bags, umbrellas, mouse pads, coffee mugs, and T-shirts, all emblazoned with the corporate name and logo. After a time you succumb to the deluge of corporate graft and begin to believe what you read. But stay strong, don't give in. Remember, taking pride in your company is like taking pride in your neighbor's son: a little creepy.

Some of the more popular slogans adorning these goodies are:

- "Putting People First"
- "Bringing Out the Gold in You"
- "We Invest in People"
- "Making a Better Workplace for You"
- "You Will Enjoy Yourself"
- "Are We Having Fun Yet? YES WE ARE!"
- "Work Harder"
- "Work Will Make You Free"

The company is shameless at branding itself through whatever means possible. Like KICK ME signs placed on the unwitting class loser, HR departments have been known to sew badges with the company motto on the jackets of unsuspecting employees. I recommend rifling through your closet right now to make sure your clothes are "clean."

BE WARY OF ANYTHING INVOLVING KILOMETERS

The 5K run, that old warhorse of corporate unity and charity work. Run five kilometers and cancer will be defeated. Disease stands no chance against the pounding of thousands of pairs of sneakers. Or so Human Resources would lead you to believe. You wake up early on a Saturday morning, slip on a T-shirt and shorts, head out to the park, and run for a half hour and everyone feels better about themselves. Or do they?

Have you ever stopped to think why corporations host these 5K walks and runs? Is it really to raise money and awareness for the disease du jour? Perhaps, if we're in a sympathetic mood. Let's stop kidding ourselves, though—you don't work for a hospital, you work for a corporation. The 5K run is a front, a means to make your company look good to the public.

So why does Human Resources sponsor events that require such immense physical exertion? Why not eat a box of cookies to fight muscular dystrophy? Or collect signatures for the "Watch TV to Fight TB" race? The average worker could at least master these activities, and most employees would participate. Why have us run 5K (and why isn't this race measured in miles?) or play softball? The answer is quite simple: Tired employees do not rebel. The strain of physical exertion depletes and enervates the worker. He barely possesses enough energy to drive to work in the morning, much less contemplate his lot in life, demand a raise, form a union, or march in a strike. He has devoted all of his energy to running for the company, unknowingly running himself into submission.

Little-known fact: From 1953 to 1967 IBM sponsored a company-wide "Bake-Off for Bronchitis." Every year the employees' wives baked a panoply of goodies, ranging from Bundt cake to fudge to cupcakes smothered in truffle sauce. The men in the gray business suits loved this time of year, and it proved a phenomenal fund-raiser. They had bronchitis back on its heels. But management noticed a growing sense of dissent among the workers. The sugars and the carbs sparked rebellious fervor among IBM's minions, culminating in the bloody food fight of '67, the last year for the bake-off. Midlevel employees rose up against execs and managers. Like a latter-day siege of the Bastille, these freedom fighters used the implements at hand to defeat the agents of oppression. Men hurled Tupperware dishes at each other, they flung toothpicks in one another's eyes, and man suffocated man with Saran Wrap. It was grisly. No one knows the exact casualty tally, since IBM never officially acknowledged this disaster. But I've talked to men who were there, who witnessed the carnage, and they claim that at least halves of dozens perished that fateful day.

The next year IBM's HR department began its "Marathon Against Male Menopause" campaign. No one has uttered a word of complaint since; employees are just too tired.

WE CAN('T) DO IT:
SUBVERTING HR MOTIVATIONAL
POSTERS

They're everywhere. Like the merciless stare of a dictator's portrait hanging in a third world country's post office, these posters and their messages bore into your soul. The hot air balloon drifting above an alpine valley with the single word "Inspiration" written in script on the bottom. Or the poster of a tiger stalking its prey, the word "Leadership" extolling you to emulate the feline's killer instinct. Ostensibly these posters are supposed to uplift and enliven you, but their actual purpose is to deaden the spirit and dull the mind. A passive employee is a malleable employee. Back in the old days, HR employed electroshock therapy and swift blows to the kneecaps to achieve those ends; now they do it through motivational posters and workshops. To be honest, I don't know which is worse. Just take a look:

- NONE OF US IS AS SMART AS ALL OF US
- DON'T AGONIZE—ORGANIZE
- PLUCK MAKES LUCK!
- FAILURE IS THE PATH OF LEAST PERSISTENCE
- CALL ON YOURSELF TO MAKE A DIFFERENCE
- POSITIVE ATTITUDE: IT CHANGES EVERYTHING!
- IF OPPORTUNITY DOESN'T KNOCK, BUILD A DOOR
- CHANGE IS GOOD

You can fight back against these insipid slogans. For beginners, I recommend the simple graffiti technique. Just add your own comments to the poster, as follows:

- 📌 KEEP ON SMILIN'—Or Else We'll Fire You.
- 📌 RISK: SOME PEOPLE DREAM—of getting out of here and moving on with their lives.

The second technique requires a bit more sophistication and a working knowledge of graphic design. Just cut and paste some photos from your booze-ridden office Christmas party and label them with the phrases "Leadership," "Keeping Our Eye on the Bottom Line," and "Lift Your Spirits." In only a few hours and with the aid of a color printer, you can collage some homemade motivational posters your coworkers will never forget.

A favorite homemade poster of mine that stayed up for an incredible three months at the office featured a photo of two monkeys humping. Beneath them it read: "Work—Get into It!" Now that's the type of creative initiative it's going to take if we want to topple the evil empire that is the Human Resources department. Good luck and Godspeed.

CHAPTER 5

IT'S ALL HIEROGLYPHICS TO ME: DECIPHERING E-MAIL

Before e-mail, companies employed ten-year-old boys to sprint from office to office, boardroom to boardroom, building to building, delivering messages of the utmost importance. True, some of these messages fell outside the purview of important communication—they were nothing more than the equivalent of today's jokey e-mail forwards—and yes, like greyhounds, a few of the boys broke down in the midst of their gallops and had to be destroyed. But when I gaze back upon those halcyon days, I find myself longing for the human element. I miss that, you know—communicating with another human being, looking another person straight in the eye and saying "Off with you now" as I rip open the manila envelope. I wonder what's happened to those prepubescent Mercurys. I have to imagine they are hobbling around on crutches, crippled by those merciless hours running on asphalt with joints and tendons not yet matured, now brittle and tender. Shame, really. You'll have to pardon my sentimentality; I fear I'm showing my age. We're no longer in the people age, we're in the digital age.

E-mail is the primary means of communication in the modern-day office. Everyone uses it and everyone seems to be using it all the time. From shooting off memos to drafting agendas to forwarding along pornographic materials, e-mail serves to satisfy a diverse array of tasks.

It can feel overwhelming at times. Hundreds of e-mails accumulate over the weekend, and by Monday morning it seems as if your job description should read: professional e-mail reader. Coming back from vacation is even worse. You will find your mailbox overflowing with URGENT and HIGH IMPORTANCE! messages. It takes all of your willpower not to chuck your computer out the window.

And then there are the emoticons, acronyms, and e-mail shorthand that grow like kudzu in each message. No one has the capability to write a traditional letter anymore. What follows is an e-mail primer that will assuage all your e-mail woes.

IS IT REALLY THAT IMPORTANT?: WHAT TO DELETE

Anything older than five days. Yes, you heard me correctly. Look under the RECEIVED tab, and anything older than five days should be deleted immediately. The East Lansing Radio Communications and Agricultural College did a study, which I sponsored, on the e-mail habits of the general worker, and they discovered this interesting nugget: If you haven't gotten to a five-day-old e-mail yet, there's a ninety percent chance you will never respond to the message.

Also delete any message preceded by the red exclamation mark that signifies "Sent with High Importance," or any e-mails with subject lines containing the words "urgent" or "read immediately." If these e-mails truly are important, the senders will either pick up the phone and call you or meet with you in person to discuss the matter. I always find it a bit presumptuous when someone feels that their e-mail is vastly more significant than the average e-mail I receive. A good rule of thumb: If you're e-mailed five times about a topic, you should respond. Otherwise, don't worry about it.

If you follow these tenets, you should never have more than half a dozen messages in your in-box.

EMOTICONS:
HOW DO YOU REALLY FEEL?

Emoticons are a way of expressing emotion through punctuation, because English does not have enough words to describe the myriad feelings coursing through our veins. Thankfully some cyber-Shakespeare discovered ":)". Without that, I don't know how I would tell someone that I am happy or pleased or in a good mood. And if I'm feeling a tad impish, I might just inject a semicolon there ";)". Here's looking at you, kid! Watch out, I got my eye on you. Just kidding!

I don't want to come across as a curmudgeon here, but as a grown man I see emoticons as the domain of teenage girls and the mentally deficient. Still, their prevalence in work-related e-mails cannot be denied, and most of your coworkers will find you a bore and a snob if you eschew them entirely. In my attempts to stay with the times, I've embraced the most popular ones and have even invented a few of my own emoticons. Because, yes, a teenage girl lurks inside even the most hardened CEO. LOL! :)

Some traditional emoticons:

:)	=	smiling
:(	=	frowning
:-D	=	laughing
:*)	=	clowning around
:-6	=	very tired
_/	=	empty glass
:-I	=	neutral, indifferent
8-)	=	dude wearing shades
<I:o)	=	smiling Santa

Here are a few more emoticons, including some I created exclusively for my company. There's no copyright restriction; appropriate these at your leisure.

:-) = Anatomically correct smiley face. People who use this emoticon are sticklers for detail. No smiley face without a nose will do for them! But where are the ears? j/k!

Just wanted to let you know that I color-coordinated all the files for the past decade as well as alphabetized the supplies in the supply room. Oh, and I installed antibacterial handwash in all the bathrooms. You can thank me with your cleanliness. :-)

:P = Tongue-sticking-out face. Can be used when you're feeling a little exasperated. It's also a cute way of saying, "Don't be such a meanie head!" One of the flirtier emoticons.

Josh! You were so mean to me at the marketing meeting. Why didn't you sit next to me?! Jerk! :P

[: = Unibrow guy. When you are feeling frazzled and need to buckle down and get some work done.

Okay, I've wasted enough time googling the hot new girl, I need to tackle this stack of reports growing on my desk. [:

%) = Googly eyes. Work overload! Help, I'm drowning in work! Somebody please sympathize with me!

Argh, argh, argh! I still have to get the numbers together for tomorrow's meeting as well as input the sales record before five. I'm losing it. %)

^ = Dunce cap. Used to note something particularly stupid said or done by management.

I'm so glad they wasted thirty mins of our morning telling us we needed to boost sales in order to increase revenue. Really? I had no idea. ^

 @ @ = Bulging eyes. When the frustration level has reached its boiling point. You can use this emoticon when addressing the object of your anger or when commenting on something particularly infuriating.

John, I needed those notes yesterday. Literally. Get on this ASAP. @ @" Or, "Ohmygod, the vending machines ran out of Skittles, what am I going to do for lunch??!? @ @ ;)

This last sentence, known as a double-e (for double emoticon), should not be attempted by those new to the form. It says, "I'm so angry about no Skittles, but hey, I also know I'm overacting just a tad—I can be a bit of a drama queen sometimes!"

BECAUSE WRITING "THANK YOU" TAKES TOO LONG: ACRONYMS AND SHORTHAND

We not only abbreviate emotions in our e-mails these days, we've also abbrev'd cumbersome phrases such as "thank you very much" and "as soon as possible." What follows is a quick and easy guide to some of the most popular acronyms and shorthand symbols. Watch in wonder as you skim seconds off your typing.

Lol	=	laugh out loud	rhts	=	raise hell this summer
fyi	=	for your information			
btw	=	by the way	glts	=	get laid this summer
asap	=	as soon as possible	scuba	=	self-contained underwater breathing apparatus
atb	=	all the best			
pdq	=	pretty damn quick			
tbd	=	to be determined	@	=	a multi-tooled symbol. It can mean "at" or "approximate" or "about."
snafu	=	situation normal all fucked up			
lylas(b)	=	love you like a sister (brother)	&	=	and
			b/c	=	because
pls	=	please	btwn	=	between
thx		thanks	t/o	=	throughout
tyvm	=	thank you very much	w/	=	with
			w/o	=	without
ttyl	=	talk to you later	w/c	=	which

Now let's put everything we've learned together in a couple of sample sentences.

McPherson, Kevin

From: jamesparker@whyarentyouemailingfaster.com
Sent: Wednesday, November 12, 10:33 A.M.
To: kevinmcpherson@ineededityesterday.com
Subject: Berkley Numbers and Spring 1998 Data Reports

Hey Kevin,

I need the Berkley numbers as soon as possible. Shoot them on over to me when you get a second. And can you also look up the data reports from Spring of '98, please?

Thanks,

James

How's it going, Wordy McWordy? They're not paying you by the word, you know. So let's make this e-mail more efficient—just sprinkle in some acronyms!

McPherson, Kevin

From: jamesparker@whyarentyouemailingfaster.com
Sent: Wednesday, November 12, 10:33 A.M.
To: kevinmcpherson@ineededityesterday.com
Subject: # spr98

K,

Need Berk #s asap. Fire away when you get a sec. & Spr. '98, pls? :)

Thx,

J

See how much time you've saved? Seconds, my friend. Precious, precious seconds.

Klimas, Carolyn

From: andrewjames@secondplaceisfirstloser.com
Sent: Friday, April 17, 3:52 P.M.
To: carolynklimas@failureisnotanoption.com
Subject: Report Question

Hi Carolyn,

Which of the two reports did you want me to send? For your information, I need them back as soon as possible. Work has been very intense these past few days. I miss you, you never call anymore, and when you write it's all about business. I still think we can salvage what we had. Call me a hopeless romantic, I don't care; what we had was too good to squander. Remember when we went self-contained underwater breathing apparatus diving? I do. I'm babbling. And I'm sad. Raise hell this summer.

All the best,

Andrew

Klimas, Carolyn

From: andrewjames@secondplaceisfirstloser.com
Sent: Friday, April 17, 3:52 P.M.
To: carolynklimas@failureisnotanoption.com
Subject: R?

C,

w/c 2 rprts? FYI, need asap. %) ;) Rmbr scuba? :(rhts.

Atb,

A

I guess e-mail shorthand does allow one to effectively communicate the mysteries of the heart. Just think of the time saved by distilling those feelings into a few quick and easy symbols! Now Carolyn and Andrew can get back to their spreadsheets and PowerPoint presentations instead of wasting time pining over what might have been.

SUBLIMINAL MESSAGES: MAKE THE LEGAL DISCLAIMER WORK FOR YOU

We've all seen the disclaimers at the ends of e-mails. The ones that state that this message is not meant to be distributed beyond the bounds of the company or used for a purpose besides a business initiative, etc.—the usual legal jargon. Most us of don't read the fine print of these disclaimers, and why should we? It's just legal department mumbo jumbo.

Even though we may not read these disclaimers, we do process them. Our eyes scan the words and our brains store them somewhere in our subconscious. This isn't David Blaine hocus-pocus, this is real life.

Advertisers have been privy to the power of subliminal thought for decades. Ever heard of those liquor ads in the sixties that fea-tured scantily clad women frozen in the ice cubes (if you look hard, you'll see them) or the cigarette ads that suggested s-e-x in the curls of the smoke? It's an old trick but an effective one. There's no reason you shouldn't update it for the digital age. How do you think I got my job? Or for that matter, my wife? Oh, yes: subliminal e-mails.

Just put in bold the appropriate letters to spell out any message you like. Perhaps you'll see a fatter paycheck because of it.

****
This e-mail **Is** the property of **W.** Consulting **Assoc.** The **coN**tents **T**herein **A**re the sole conce**R**n of the p**A**rtners. **If** thi**S** m**E**ssage does **N**ot reach its intended **O**bject please return to **W.** Consulting. Thank you.
****

If you have success with this beginner's exercise, you might want to attempt something more advanced. Below is what I consider the *Hamlet* of subliminal e-mail messages.

Demblowski, Matt

From:	dwmartin@superiorleadershipskills.com
Sent:	Friday, July 10, 2:28 P.M.
To:	mattdemblowski@showmethemoney.com
Subject:	BBQ

Hi Matt,

Just a quick note to see how you're doing. Looking forward to the BBQ this weekend. Thanks for just being you.

Best,

DW

****
This e-mail is the property of W. Consulting Group. The contents therein are the sole **GIVE** concern of listen Matt I'm miserable right now all alone unable to find someone the partners **ME** and employees of you know how the singles scene is it's just a meat
****

market and yeah I love **YOUR** playing the field I have no regrets that for the past five years I woke up next to complete strangers **WIFE** but it's time I grew up and I just see you and Mary Beth and how happy you are and that's **PLEASE** what W. Consulting Group and any attempt to forward this material on I want a family and **THANKS** the joy of coming home to someone after a hard day's work I want what you have and I want you to hand over your wife at the BBQ this weekend thanks bro you're a real *team player* will be dealt with by the legal department.

Seem like too much work? Not when you consider the payoff. Mary Beth and I have enjoyed three years of marriage together; I wouldn't trade it for the world. Matt still doesn't know what hit him, but joining AA has helped put him back on track.

Use subliminal messages for any variety of needs and watch your dreams become reality.

THE ART OF VOICE MAIL: HOW TO MUMBLE YOUR NUMBER SO THEY NEVER CALL BACK

A recent innovation I do applaud is voice mail. Once upon a time you had to talk to everyone who dialed your number; you could not avoid the misfits, the yellers, or the marathon talkers for risk of missing an important phone call. With voice mail you know that if you call someone during lunch, you'll get the machine and be home free. Or if you're on the East Coast and need to call somebody in L.A., call when you first get into work, and those of you on the West Coast should place your calls at the end of the workday. You'll never have to talk to another boring or abusive or long-winded client again.

There are also times when the person you are calling is so awful that you don't want them to ever call you back. Maybe you're begrudgingly doing a favor for an associate, or maybe you know that a returned call will only create more work for yourself and little payback. You should harbor no guilt about avoiding these people. Just garble your number on their machine and rest easy knowing you will never have to speak to them.

Below are a few ways to leave a professionally indecipherable phone number:

 Put marbles in your mouth. Simple, almost childish, but effective. And if for some reason the person picks up the phone, you can always use the "just got back from the dentist" excuse.

 Give an incomplete number. Can be lots of fun imagining the person trying all the different combinations as they vainly attempt to call you back.

 Give your number multiple times, but change it slightly each time. Example: "Okay, so just give me a call when you get this. My number is 323-5, no, wait, I guess you'll need the area code, huh? So it's 212-323-46, nope, that's the fax, sorry about that. All right, it's 212-323-64, hold it . . . we just got new numbers, that's the old one. 212-323-56, I mean 65." Trust me, they will have crossed out the various digits so many times they'll give up on calling you back.

Carry on another conversation as you leave your number. Just pretend you are having a conversation with a colleague: "Call me back at 212—What, Cliff? Yeah, I'll send over those numbers to you right away . . . 32 . . . No, it was batch 48 they wanted, third row over, second down . . . Sorry about that, where was I? 212-323 . . . 678 . . . That's the sales fig you're looking for . . . Ah, 64 . . . 521 was the old number . . . 84 . . . Sorry about all the confusion. So just give me a call when you get a chance." You get the idea. Just recite all the numbers at a rapid speed.

I have tested these methods innumerable times. They're fool-proof. Have fun eluding the undesirables of the business world.

CHAPTER 6

WOWING THEM IN THE BOARDROOM: HOW TO MASTER THE BIG MEETING

The key to a successful career lies in how you manage the big meeting. Your success derives partly from handling the pressure of an important presentation and partly from your adroitness at parrying the feints and thrusts of a verbal disagreement. But the truly savvy businessperson has the ability to talk up ideas without taking on any of the actual responsibility. My mantra is: Create, then delegate.

Whenever I counsel my young executives on how to handle themselves in a meeting, I always tell them the boardroom is like an ex-wife: difficult to please, unwilling to listen to new ideas, concerned only with outward appearances, and looking to humiliate you the moment you slip up. What follows is a surefire, can't-miss plan to winning the war of words at your next boardroom meeting. Follow these tips and climb to the top of the heap.

VERB IT!:
CREATE YOUR OWN VERBS

Verbs convey power, decisiveness, and initiative—all traits that a boardroom finds attractive. And verbs are easy to make up—don't feel obligated to use the ones already in common use. Be daring, be different, test the elasticity of the English language and conjure up your own verbs.

Just add a suffix like "-ed" or "-ize" to the end of any word, and you have yourself a verb. It's really that simple. Sure, English teachers may balk at your creativity, but you're not working for the English department, you're working for people who've made something of themselves, and they'll be duly *impressedatized* with your initiative. Here are some examples of how you can incorporate new verbs into your business talk:

- **"I memoed the memo to your assistant."** Redundancy makes you seem like an even more conscientious worker. Always be redundant. Redundancy really drives the point home. You can never be too redundant when it comes to redundancy.
- **"The Briggs account is in the bag. I circ'd the paperwork for sig, cc'd the prez, and distro'd the forms to the accounting dept."** Notice that I abbrev'd the verbs—it's an advanced technique and quite effective.
- **"I Lexis-Nexised the company's profits, Googled all the major players, and websitalized all the pertinent figures."** That just means you did research and posted your findings on the intranet, but doesn't it sound impressive?

Other possible verbs to use:

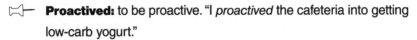 **Proactived:** to be proactive. "I *proactived* the cafeteria into getting low-carb yogurt."

Profitized: to make a profit. "We *profitized* thirty percent from the Cheetos ad campaign."

Memoize: to write a memo or, if you have a speech impediment, to commit something to memory (I'm just being cute there). "I *memoized* the new dress code and will talk about enforcement in the managers' meeting."

Disked: to save to a disk. "I *disked* the sales presentation."

Reverbiagize: to restate or reword a proposal after the initial proposal was denied. "Don't worry about coming up with a new idea, we'll just *reverbiagize* the old one."

Watercoolered: to spread gossip. "I *watercoolered* the news that Cliff got *pink-slipped*."

Pink-slipped: to get fired; see above.

Cubicled: to get demoted. "Did you hear about Barry? Yeah, pretty pathetic, they *cubicled* him back in sales."

Remember, companies want to exist on the precipice of the next big thing. They crave innovative employees, and what better way to prove your mettle than by transforming the English language? Merriam-Websterize your way to the top!

Furniturespeak:
This Old Boardroom

When it comes to business phrases, inspiration can oftentimes come from the most prosaic of sources: the office decor. Ever since Caesar told Brutus to "slab this discussion for later" ("slab" being Roman for "table"), business leaders have looked to their surroundings to convey what they really mean. Below is a list of commonly used "furniturespeak" terms. These are great to pull out in boardroom meetings—referencing the ceiling, the floor, the chairs, the windows, or the table gives your bored coworkers a point of reference.

Frame the argument.
Trash that idea.
Are you *plugged* into this discussion?
Let me *couch* it in these terms.
Shelve that item for later.
We have a short *window* of opportunity on this.
It's *curtains*!
We've hit a *wall*.
Can you shed some *light* on this matter?
Frank is going to hit the *ceiling* when he gets this report.

Tom has the *floor* right now.
Can you *chair* the meeting?
Let's take that idea off the *table*.
The shit has hit the *fan*.

MAKE IT HAPPEN, PEOPLE

But enough with the abstract. Below are some common real-life boardroom situations where you will have to be on your toes to succeed. Follow these pointers and you'll be kickin' some gray flannel ass in no time. In fact, do you smell something? Because I do. It's that tangy raise you're about to receive.

In every meeting there is that lone wolf who takes it upon himself or herself to criticize and question every statement you make. The next time he or she speaks out against you, just respond with, "Robert, thanks for driving home your point, but you need to agendize these thoughts before you mention them at the meeting. Just interoffice your ideas to me afterward and when I get a sec I'll take them into account. By the by, have you gained some weight? Looking a little chunky round the middle, aren't we?"

With strong words such as these, your nemesis will cower in the face of your linguistic pyrotechnics. Congratulations: You've power-played your first face-off.

After anyone raises any point at all in a meeting, ask, "But how will that affect our profit marginalization ratio? I don't think anyone wants to take a bath on this one."

The sentence means little, but you used a key word—"profit"—and seemed to express concern about the ability to make said profit. Can a company ask for a more devoted employee?

When a coworker submits a jargon-heavy explanation of something, simply reply, "In English . . . please."

Ha! Oh, the irony. Even though you yourself engage in office-speak, by being the first one to point out the need to cut through all the corporate BS and get right to the crux of the matter, you make it almost impossible for anyone to call you out on your own meaningless chatter. You're a straight shooter and your colleagues will eat that up.

INTERRUPT, INTERRUPT, INTERRUPT

One of the keys to gaining your coworkers' respect is to be a good listener. Other people have ideas to contribute, and they want to know that their contributions receive the same consideration as yours. Unfortunately, every time someone else is speaking you are left with less time to make an impact—hence the importance of mastering the fine art of interrupting. There are numerous ways to interrupt. Let's begin with the most polite methods:

"Good point." Your colleague is prattling on and on about how he has discovered some inefficiencies within the company and has come up with alternative solutions to streamline the process. As he pauses to inhale, you blurt out "good point" at a rapid-fire pace. Your "good points" will mow him down before he can regain composure, leaving you free to take the floor.

"Interesting . . ." Unlike "good point," "interesting" is most commonly used when a good point is clearly not being made. No need to wait for a pause, just interrupt midsentence and let the word "interesting" slip out of your mouth like jam onto a scone. Everyone knows that what you're really saying is, "Shut the hell up, you irrelevant moron."

"I like what you're saying, but let's discuss this offline." This is the quintessential affable blowoff. Although you have no interest in the point being made and are annoyed that your colleague is prolonging an already tedious meeting, this phrase is a much gentler way of conveying that sentiment.

Sometimes, though, expressing yourself politely doesn't get the job done, and you have to take a more aggressive approach. Some of the following suggestions may feel awkward the first few times you attempt them. But trust me, once you get the hang of them, you'll be itching for any opportunity to interrupt.

"Can we move on?" A more confrontational stance—one that is best used with those who work below you.

 Fake a violent cough. Apologize for interrupting and then segue into your own personal agenda. The glob of phlegm hanging from your chin will distract your coworkers and silence the room. Works like a charm.

 "Oh my God, I think my water broke." Even if you're not pregnant and especially if you're not a woman, don't be afraid to use this one. All conversation immediately terminates as nervous colleagues contemplate having to actually help someone.

 "BOOORRRIIINNNGGG!" Say this as you yawn and make a stretching motion. Then start picking your fingernails and exclaim, "How fascinating!"

 "For God's sake, are you done yet?" If you're thinking it, odds are that everyone else is too.

 "Is the top of your head loose? Because I think a dog pried it open and crapped in it." Vulgar? Undoubtedly. But fun to say? Unquestionably. (Also appropriate for use at family gatherings.)

HYBRID WORDS

Hybrid words will play an integral role throughout your career. Whether you're making a presentation, pitching a concept to a client, or just shooting the breeze with a colleague over coffee, hybrid words add élan to your speech. They make you sound important, imposing, and imperious—the three big "im" words. File these hybrids away, write them on Post-it notes and sticker your house, do whatever it takes to memorize these words. Remember, if you sound important, you are important.

"Synergy" stakes its claim to being the first business-oriented hybrid word, and we'll grant it that. But there is a whole slew of hybrids out there and many more to be invented. Like hybrid species, hybrid words are the future of our society.

- **Actioneering:** to be proactive, to engineer a plan. "We need to get *actioneering* on the Givens campaign or else we'll never meet our deadline."
- **Bloatware:** unneccessary, cumbersome software that causes more problems than it solves. "The IT department just installed the new office management *bloatware* on my computer. The hard drive always crashes now, and they blocked my access to eBay."
- **Infotainment:** relating corporate news in a fun, fresh manner. Think *Access Hollywood.* It'll be the first time anyone has ever contemplated *Access Hollywood*. "Our sales presentation needs to be one part fact and nine parts *infotainment* to keep everyone from falling into a coma. Do you think Billy Bush is available?"
- **Europrofitization:** the profit gained from backpacking through Europe. "My *europrofitization* involved seeing the Eiffel Tower and sneaking home a bag of hash."

Agressarket: to market aggressively. "We need to *agressarket* this sugar water to seventh graders everywhere."

Wasteformation: useless information. "It came as no surprise to anyone that the monthly Human Resources newsletter was full of *wasteformation*."

Stratteger: strategy letter. "Lynn, would you please draw up a *stratteger* for me about how to increase productivity in our Southeast Asia markets?"

Failurestone: opposite of a milestone. "The day we hired Gary was a *failurestone* for this company. Revenues declined by fifty percent, and the toilets were always clogged."

Suspishareholders: shareholders who actually inquire about how a company accounts for its revenues. "The last thing we need, Harold, are a bunch of *suspishareholders* prying into our books. They need to be stopped. Permanently."

Use these genetically engineered words to devastating effect at your next meeting. Then watch with glee as your colleagues frantically try to overtake the steep learning curve that is the art of the hybrid.

SORRY, I'M SWAMPED:
THE ART OF DELEGATING

It's important to treat the boardroom like your lover. Control the dialogue, use words to confuse the situation to your benefit, be forceful, never take "no" for an answer, and if necessary, put sedatives in the water.

Part of taking control is creating, then delegating. I'm too important a person to do all the busywork I create, and I imagine you are as well. But since you initiated the work, it is only natural for your colleagues to assume that you will bear the brunt of the pencil pushing—the fools. Below are some time-honored methods to redirect your workload:

Flattery

I don't normally recommend praising a coworker. Why say something good about someone when you can say something good about yourself? However, this is an ideal time to shine the spotlight on those sedulous, ambitious colleagues of yours. "Listen, I'd love to research those thousand databases I mentioned, but I just don't think I'm the man for the job. Laura actually told me just the other day that she wished she were on the Internet more often. Remember that, Laura? This seems like the perfect project for you."

And there you have it—Laura's got the job and you've made a new friend through your magnanimous act.

"I'm Swamped."

The classic phrase. No one ever argues with someone who pleads "swampedness."

Boss: "Hey, you, great idea about personally contacting our 350 vendors. Nothing like making that one-on-one connection. When do you think you can get to that?"

You: "Oh, thanks for thinking of me to head up this project. I'm flattered [excellent use of reverse flattery] and I'd love to do it [always stress how much you would love to undertake a project], but I'm swamped right now. However, I think Albert would be perfect for the job. I've heard him on the telephone on numerous occasions and I'm wowed by his technique. Incredible, Al. That whole 'catch you on the flip' and calling guys 'germs' is great stuff. It's all yours, buddy. Run with it."

And don't forget to take all the credit once they've finished doing the grunt work. After all, it was your idea. Anyone can crunch numbers, but only a gifted few can create work opportunities for others.

These are the basic tools you need to dominate the boardroom. I've supplied you with the wrench, awl, and band saw, and now it's up to you to not slice off your hand as you reach for corporate glory.

True Story: Playing Cribbage with Warren Buffett

My favorite place to watch a sunset is from the gazebo on my pala-
tial resort in Barbados. I have my own rum distillery on the grounds,
naturally, and I find that nothing goes better with jerked goat than a

rum and Coke. Well, that and the presence of my dear friend Warren Buffett, a regular at Dominion Colony. As two villagers massaged our necks during our last stay and stuffed dates into our mouths while we played a fierce game of cribbage, I asked Warren, "So, how did you handle yourself in the boardroom? Were you a listener? A yeller? A stern boss? Or a friend?" He moved a peg, chewed his date, and replied, "I listened and let people dig their own graves. Don't talk just to hear the sound of your own voice." Silence filled the room as we exchanged knowing smiles. I shall never forget that dusky game of cribbage nor the beatific look on Warren's face as date juice sluiced down his chin.

You've conquered the boardroom, but how will you fare around the all-important watercooler? Light another Gauloises cigarette and turn the page.

CHAPTER 7

I'LL TAKE MINE ON THE ROCKS: THE LANGUAGE OF THE WATERCOOLER

Up until now we have dealt only with the professional aspect of officespeak—how to converse in the boardroom and in the interview, how to muffle a voice mail message—but we have yet to delve into the social side of officespeak. Your eight hours in the office are as much social as they are business. And for some of you, if not most of you, socializing predominates. It's like high school all over again, except you're stuck at the same desk for the entire day and you don't have a ponytailed guidance counselor telling you to follow your heart. Although if you work at some testosterone-infused consulting firm, you still might have to worry about swirlies.

But you do have pep rallies in the guise of corporate retreats, you still pray for the occasional snow day, and no one enjoys staying late at work. As in high school, much of your success is inextricably linked to whom you know. Repeat after me: Choose your friends wisely. Just because someone has a great personality and always has something positive to say doesn't mean he or she is good friend material. When first encountering a new person, ask yourself: "What can he or she do for me?" Is it really worth your time making small talk with a colleague who just wants to go out for drinks after work and have a good time? Doubtful. Those people are a dime a dozen, and they have a front-row seat on the highway to failure. No, better to associate with the cutthroats in the office, those who would gladly sell their mothers to a Thai organ harvester for a quick buck. I don't mean to paint a bleak and Hobbesian view of the office, but we're all grown-ups here. We know how it works. You can have unambitious friends who are always there for you, sure, but when push comes to shove, you need to be prepared to send them hurtling into oncoming traffic. The only thing standing between you and the corner office is your social life.

This chapter will teach you the key phrases you need to ingratiate yourself with those who matter, while at the same time not alienating the little people. Because every leader needs followers.

BACK TO BASICS:
SO HOW WAS YOUR WEEKEND?

The most commonly asked question in the office, besides "God, you look like shit, what happened to you?" is "How was your weekend?" It's the multi-anything phrase. Whether you're mucking it up with the executives or showing that you're just one of the guys with the mail room folk, this question applies to everyone. Why? Simple: because everybody had a weekend, and most people have an opinion about that weekend even if it's just "All right."

Yet come Wednesday (or "hump day") asking your colleagues how their weekend was will truly make it seem like you don't care. You've had two days to ferret out this information, and people will begin to wonder why you didn't ask earlier. This is where you begin phase two of your casual conversation lesson: "What are you doing *this* weekend?" Most people do not want to discuss their work lives. People live for the weekend and the splendors it holds: movies, bars, and regretful sexual relations. The vast majority of human beings consider Monday through Friday a five-day roadblock to the weekend, so you can't fail when steering conversations to those activities taking place on Saturday and Sunday.

Always appear keenly interested as your colleague recounts some "crazy" story about the bar he went to and how he got so "shit-faced" that he fell asleep on the dance floor. "Whoa, that is crazy, Pete! You slept on the dance floor?! Dude, you were blitzed. Keep it real, rock star, I have to make some copies." Such support of blatantly juvenile behavior will solidify your reputation as "just one of the guys."

Sometimes you will be asked how your weekend was in return. There are numerous ways to respond, ranging from honesty to an elaborate lie involving a winning lottery ticket, a brisk wind, and a fateful sewer grate. The best response should make you appear a tad intriguing; you want people talking about you in the office.

For example:

You: Hey, Stacy, how was your weekend?
Stacy: Okay. Well, actually pretty bad. My dog, Max, has been really sick and I had to put him down. And you?

You: Wow. Sorry. [Sympathetic pause.] My weekend was fine. Didn't do much, you know, just went to the UN and planted a tracking device on the Austrian ambassador. Then went clubbing in the Hamptons with Carly Simon. The usual. Well, catch you later. Sorry about your dog.

In and out, you feigned making a connection. Textbook. Now she'll think of you as not only that sensitive person who empathized about her dog, but more importantly, as someone with a high-powered, possibly life-threatening, social life.

Besides the above technique, you can also comment on the speed with which the weekend passed. Most of your colleagues are convinced that the forty-eight hours between Friday and Sunday night are shorter than any forty-eight-hour time span during the workweek. Always stress the briskness of the weekend, a favorite conversation topic that works with everyone from the CEO to the security guard:

📌 "They should just give us three-day weekends permanently, don't you think? I would be so much more productive at work if I had that extra day off."

📌 "At least Martin Luther King Day is only three weeks away."

📌 "Back to the grind. It never ends, does it?"

📌 "Man, it just flew by. One minute I'm doing Jell-O shots off some limbo girl and the next minute I wake up in a bathtub full of ice. Craziness."

📌 "Why do I come back? Oh dear God, why have you given me this life?"

Bonus Fun Talk

When taking the elevator, comment that you must be on the "local" if it stops at every floor. This gets a knowing laugh and designates you as the "office wit."

POP CULTURE: THAT MADONNA SURE IS SOMETHING, HUH?

If people aren't talking about the weekend or complaining about their boss, they are probably discussing the latest reality television show or newest Hollywood blockbuster. It's difficult to keep up with all the entertainment offerings out there, but you don't want to seem out of touch. And while the latest pop sensation seems to change as often as my nephew's sheets (he's a chronic bed wetter, much to the family's embarrassment, and no amount of public humiliation seems able to shame him into stopping), it takes just a little effort to be on top of the latest pop culture offerings.

Go to your newsstand and pick up a copy of *Us Weekly*. Swallow your pride. If I can do it, you can do it. Not that I've ever seen child pornography, but I have to imagine that the shame and self-loathing felt when looking at such material must be similar to the general sense of disgust that spreads through my body as I leaf through page after page of celebrity fashion do's and don'ts and the primer on hot new dresses for this year's Oscars. If you are not familiar with *Us Weekly,* it's a magazine that makes *USA Today* look like a legitimate news source. It traffics in the inane and the celebrity obsessed, and it is your best guide to keeping afloat amidst pop culture chatter. This may seem like small stuff, and don't get me wrong, it is; but you never know when this knowledge could provide you with just the "in" you were looking for with a certain high-level executive.

If you fall behind in your pop reading, don't worry. Nothing becomes dated faster than the "it" people and shows. Well, maybe JLo dates faster. (Sorry, I had to. Ben Affleck and I spot each other while doing leg lifts at the gym; he's good people—she's hurt a lot of decent men.) No matter what, these ten phrases will make you seem like a pop culture maven and should last for the next five years. By then my next magnum opus, *The Lost Treasure of Officespeak,* will be on the shelves and it will feature the next batch of celebrity references with which to wow your coworkers. Meanwhile, drop these lines whenever you want to impress colleagues with your pop culture prowess. Remember, knowing a lot about unimportant things such as TV, movies, and pop music makes you likeable. No one likes a career-driven culture snob, so mask that side of yourself with these bon mots:

- "When are the two Coreys [Feldman and Haim] going to get their act together and make *License to Drive 2*?"

- *"Fear Factor* is nuts. They have to eat bugs on that show! TV's awesome!"

- "Can you believe the crazy thing Jessica Simpson said? She's duuummmbbb. Or is she?"

- "I really like when celebrities voice their political opinions. They are so wise."

- "I'm glad to see Will Smith is taking full advantage of his talents by making another movie where he attacks aliens and robots."

- "Gwyneth [Paltrow] is so elegant and smart. I hope she gets elected Queen of the World."

- "How hot are the Olsen twins, dude? Are they eighteen yet?"

- "When is Michael Jackson going to stop touching boys? At this rate the pope's going to make him a cardinal." (Include a rimshot sound effect after delivering this surefire one-liner. Trust me, people can't get enough of the Michael Jackson jokes. Good times.)

- "Nicole Kidman is not bony enough."

- "I can't wait to see that new movie in which stuff explodes a lot and things catch on fire."

- EXTRA TIP: "Simon Cowell is so mean. I can't believe what he said. British people should be shot."

NICKNAMES:
FOR THOSE TIMES WHEN THE
REAL NAMES ELUDE YOU, CHAMP

Give your coworkers nicknames like "rock star," "superstar," or "dawg." People love nicknames; they lend an air of intimacy where there probably is none. Other simple nickname devices: Take the person's first initial and tack it onto the beginning of his or her last name. For example, Brian Richards would be "Brichards." Or add an *s* to the end of the first syllable of the first name. For instance: Sally would be "Sals" and Michael would be "Mikes." There are endless variations on this theme; I just wanted to provide the kindling to ignite the nickname brushfire in your imagination. If someone looks like a particular animal, call him or her by that animal's name. If someone has a distinguishing feature like a hunched back or lots of cellulite, call that out as well. Have some fun. I had an assistant who had horrible acne, the kind of stuff that not even tetracycline can clear up. We would call him "Zitface," "Polka dot," "Braillehead," "Crusty," and a whole lot more. We had a blast coming up with new ones, and I know the nicknames fostered a great sense of unity in the office. Nicknames also prove useful when you've forgotten somebody's actual name. Using "sport," "tiger," and "hey, you" will keep the person from discovering that you have no idea what his or her real name is.

THE BUSINESS OF FRIENDSHIP:
THE KEYS TO NETWORKING

Networking is an officespeak word used to describe making friends with those who will help you climb the corporate ladder; it is the key to your success in any industry. Don't hesitate to ingratiate—that's what I tell the people who shell out $1,500 to attend one of my weekend seminars. Kissing ass and brownnosing may still possess the stigma it carried in high school, but what do you care if people talk about you behind your back? You'll be the one who landed the sweet new job because of casual acquaintances in high places!

How do you know if one of your peers is a player? How do you separate the future CEOs from the future soccer moms and family men? Keep an eye out for the person always willing to take on extra work, someone who feeds on pressure. Look for a colleague who belittles his peers and threatens violence against those who question his ideas. If someone uses the following phrases, you're witnessing a future Michael Milken.

 "I needed those figures yesterday. Jesus, how did you get a job here?"

 "We must pulverize the competition. Make them cry like orphans."

"Life? What life? My life is the company and making money. Hobbies and wives are for those who forgot to grow testicles."

Once you've picked your marks, investigate them. Put on your sleuthing cap: Do a Google search, see where they went to school and what organizations they belonged to. The Internet is an awesome resource, and it can be used for much good, as well as for prying into people's pasts. Pry away. Then drop into casual conversation something like, "I don't know if you're familiar with Harvard, but there is no more inspiring place than the Yard in autumn." Or "Don't laugh, but I still find myself yearning for those glee club days back in college" or just spontaneously start singing the person's school fight song and bashfully say, "Sorry, couldn't help myself, I bleed [insert school colors]." Watch his mouth drop open when you claim to be a member of the same fraternity. No need to worry about showing any proof—just recite this story and they'll leave well enough alone: "Dude, I wish I could remember my frat days, you know what I mean? The only thing I do know is that I got this chick preggers and we threw the baby down a well. Browser, I was insane."

Listen to what your new friend says in meetings—the phrases, the ideas he generates. If he says things like "Do you read me?" "That's on my radar screen," and "rectal database," throw those office-speak terms back at him when you're outside of the boardroom. Demonstrate to him that you follow his every word; imitation is the greatest form of flattery. Who cares if he's an obnoxious, shallow, corporate raider—this scum of the earth just might land you your dream job.

Now you've made a work friend. Use him for all he's worth.

NICE ASS:
COMPLIMENTING YOUR COWORKERS

We live in a new era. Once upon a time a man could smack his secretary on her bum and tell her she looked good and no one would bat an eye. It was just a means of being social, a way of saying, "Hey, how are you doing? Oh and by the way, I really appreciate the heft and curvature of your ass." Those were the days of martini shakers, Frank Sinatra songs, fedoras, unfiltered cigarettes, and cars without seat belts. Men were men and women were women, and the only way men knew how to communicate affection for the opposite sex was by touching the body part that they admired.

But then the seventies and Gloria Steinem and women's liberation happened, and all of a sudden women wanted to be treated with respect. As if encomiums from a boss regarding a woman's physical appearance is somehow offensive. Listen, ladies, it's not our fault you look so damn good. And it ain't our fault that we have to tell you how fine you really is. If men did not possess the "compliment gene" (as I like to call it), then Adam would not have "hooked up" with Eve and we would not be here having this discussion. Kind of makes you think, doesn't it?

Even so, times have changed, and that type of behavior is no longer deemed acceptable. When I was told I couldn't squeeze the bosom of a coworker or assure a promotion in exchange for sexual favors, I almost quit the business entirely. Why wake up each morning if the promise of sexual release could no longer blossom, like a rare orchid, amidst the hothouse of the office? I am a botanist, if you will, not a machine.

But, like a chair, we must all adjust. Andrew Carnegie confided in me over a couple of Long Island iced teas that the most difficult concession he ever made was taking down his prized collection of dildos. Into every life a little rain must fall.

Nowadays you'll be fired for any inappropriate contact you make or for any "demeaning and derogatory comments" you utter. The battlefield of the heart, already dangerous terrain, is now littered with verbal minefields.

Here is a list of words no longer considered appropriate when addressing female colleagues: "broad," "dame," "bimbo," "floozy," "babycakes," "hot momma," "dirty girl," "bitch," "whore," "slut." Instead female coworkers must be referred to as "her" or "that woman" or "lady friend." You can no longer admire a particularly lovely female by saying, "Nice tits" or "What an ass." Restrictive? Yes. Imagine visiting the Sistine Chapel and being told that it is forbidden to gaze in awe at Michelangelo's supreme achievement or to utter the words "glorious," "awesome," "life-altering," "splendiferous." That'll give you a sense of what it's like for men to operate in the twenty-first-century office.

If you must compliment a woman, be cautious. They are deceptive creatures. Say something like "nice hair" or "interesting eyes." They like when you notice their hair and eyes. Otherwise discuss the weather and what they plan to make for dinner that evening.

I apologize if this section alienates the female readership or if it appears too slanted toward the male perspective. But you have to understand that men would love to be sexually harassed. It's a quiet dream of ours. Please pinch our butts, stare at our groins, post dirty pictures in our cubicles, call us "lust stallion" and "keeper of the manthrone." We don't mind being objectified. Honest. Then and only then will we bridge this seemingly unbridgeable gap between the sexes.

OFFICE TYPES

Every office contains a number of people who no one wants to talk to. Like the kid in school who never showered or the girl who had to wear headgear all the time, these people are social pariahs. The following is a list of those coworkers you should avoid. I've included descriptions and sample dialogue to help you identify these office lepers. Engage them in conversation at your own risk.

The Martyr

No one works harder or more unselfishly than the Martyr. Or at least according to the Martyr. The Martyr sloughs down the hallway with back bent from all the extra work he shoulders for the department, eyes half-closed from lack of sleep; a low groan, like the death call of a goat, can be heard rumbling from his chest as he skulks past your cubicle. The Martyr's salutation is always a sigh, a mournful, creaking sigh. You may find it difficult to control your frustration when dealing with the Martyr. Everyone has work to do, but most of us don't go around crying about it.

- "You're so lucky to be able to leave at five. I can't remember the last time I left on time. First to arrive, last to leave, story of my life."
- "I'll try to get to that . . . on Saturday."
- "Don't worry about me, I've got it under control. I'll just have to stay late again. My wife must think I'm a stranger when she sees me!"
- "Wow, your pictures from Hawaii are incredible. I haven't gone on a vacation in ten years. You're so lucky not to have so much work to do."
- "Oh no, don't thank *me* or anything."
- "Entering all the sales data is fun. And carpal tunnel syndrome is kind of a badge of honor, right?"
- "My hair falls out in patches in the morning. I lost twelve pounds last week. Sure, I can cover for you."

The Stalker

You don't have to be a celebrity to warrant the affections of a stalker. You don't even have to be attractive. You just have to have made the mistake of being nice to the most socially awkward person in the office. Now that person has Googled and Friendstered you and constructed a fantasy social life in which the two of you go for picnics and rows on the lake and watch classic *Star Trek* episodes late into the gloaming. Most likely the Stalker has constructed a shrine for you at his or her own house. This shrine contains personal possessions of yours, ranging from a lock of hair to a snotty used tissue you threw away. Notes you scribbled onto Post-its, doodles made in the margins of handouts and then put in the recycling bin, all become fuel for the Stalker's obsession. The Stalker probably won't harm you, and at first you might even be flattered by all the attention (as creepy as it might be), but after a while this relationship could damage your office reputation.

The Stalker possesses a magical ability to appear whenever you least expect him. Say when you're working late and you go to the copier and discover the Stalker making copies of fliers for the upcoming Renaissance fair. Or you race for an elevator, barely beating the closing doors, and suddenly an arm pushes through and in walks the Stalker. Sometimes the Stalker is sitting in the toilet stall right next to yours. Yes, the Stalker is everywhere.

If and when the Stalker musters the nerve to talk to you, the conversation will consist mainly of weird smiles and halting attempts to ask you about your favorite TV show. Here are some other phrases that are part of the Stalker's dossier. When reading these statements, picture an overweight man with greasy, stringy black hair, acne, and the remnants of Chicken McNuggets stuck between his teeth:

⟋ "I think you're pretty."

⟋ "We need to hang out. Like all the time."

⟋ "Pretty hair, pretty hair. Soft, pretty hair. I like to smell your hair late at night."

⟋ "You're the only one who is nice to me. We should get married."

⟋ "I watched you last night. That man in your house seems mean. I don't like him."

⟋ "I'm writing a book called *The Elves of Zanx.* Princess Qu'rit is based on you."

⟋ "Why are you walking away? Don't walk away. I give nice hugs."

You can try the nice route when first confronted by the Stalker, but that ultimately only encourages him. The best way to deal with the Stalker is with a cold shoulder and a taser gun.

The Talker

Every office has the Talker. The guy who wanders the halls and meanders about the cubicles, offices, and copier centers looking for anyone who will listen. The Talker knows everything and can discourse on any subject for any length of time to anyone. Some of his favorite topics include award shows, entertainment trivia, compiling of lists (all-time best sequels, Led Zeppelin albums, concert T-shirts, etc.), military campaigns, and the "insane" forwards he got from his buddies that morning. The Talker also enjoys skipping down his own personal memory lane for you: indulging in "outrageous" frat initiation stories, a legendary high school athletic career, and the "twisted" exploits of his European backpacking trip with his college buddy Trevor and a German neofascist named Klieg. If he feels particularly close to you, he might even reveal a vulnerable side to himself, such as being held back in the third grade or not having a date to his senior prom. The Talker has a good heart, but even you have to admit that work needs to be done sometimes.

 "Hey, let me ask you something real quick. *Godfather I* or *II*?" (Your response, either way, will lead to a fifteen-minute monologue.)

 "I don't know how familiar you are with World War II, but I was just watching this documentary on the History Channel on Saturday, and did you know that Patton wanted to invade Soviet Russia at the conclusion of the war? Pretty gutsy move. Makes you think, what if he did that, you know?"

 "Okay, I need you to settle a bet. My buddy and I have a Pizza Hut Stuffed Crust Pizza on the line here: Who's hotter, Elizabeth Berkley or Tiffani-Amber Thiessen?"

 "Why don't you think *Dark Side of the Moon* is better than *Zeppelin 3*? I really want to talk about this."

 "Did you go to your senior prom? Because I didn't. The girl I had this huge crush on was dating the quarterback, complete cliché. Then she broke up with him in March and I was, you know, like, about to make my move. But she got into this drunk driving accident. She wasn't drunk or anything, but the driver of the car was, and she was in a coma and really cut up so, you know, obviously she couldn't make it to prom. That sucked."

 "You won't believe what Trevor, Klieg, and I did when we were in Munich. Ohmygod. We drank so much beer and then looted this old graveyard place. *In*sane."

Warning: The Talker can morph into the Stalker. Red flags should go up once he starts prying into your love life and when he admits that while Ted Bundy did do some bad things he was, by all accounts, a "nice guy."

The Dieter

The Dieter makes everyone feel uncomfortable. Although most likely a woman, the Dieter can be that rare male who actually cares about his weight. The Dieter fusses over every last crumb at every office function, telling everyone within a ten-foot radius, "Oh, no, I shouldn't have eaten all of that. Guess you guys will hear me coming down the hallway tomorrow, huh?" The Dieter needs constant reassurance that she is not heavy, that she looks great, and that it's okay to indulge sometimes. And most of the time she does look great. There's absolutely nothing wrong with her besides her bundle of insecurities.

But the Dieter's greatest accomplishment is to make the women around her feel like slobs. She comments on how incredibly thin they are, yet repeatedly points out how much they consume, hinting at a possible eating disorder tucked away in the bathroom stall. She loves counting calories, especially other people's calories. If you didn't have an eating disorder before encountering the Dieter, you probably will have one afterward.

- "Does anybody want to split this carrot with me?"
- "I'm just eating celery this week. That's all! Nothing but celery. And look, I'm still going to gain ten pounds!"
- "You're so brave to eat that cupcake. It has so much fat! But I guess you don't have to worry about that."
- "You are so thin and you eat so much. I hate you. I hate you. Just kidding! Ha ha ha! I love you."
- "Another weekend without a date. No surprise, who'd want to date a fatty like me?"
- "Maybe I should take a course in anorexia. Just kidding!"

True Story: Heartbreak with Martha Stewart

In the early nineties I had a torrid affair with Martha Stewart. My wife had yet to shed her pregnancy weight, and I began to look elsewhere for companionship. A mutual friend introduced us at a fabric store (this was my lace phase), and what started as a business partnership quickly melted into a bedroom partnership.

We sequestered ourselves at my kingdom by the sea in the South Pacific, seeking solace from the cold, harsh world we knew. In a way, you could say we mutinied from the HMS *Life*.

We made desperate, unquenchable love. Like two castaways stranded on a remote island with only rudimentary means of converting salt water to fresh water, we quivered to drink in the pure H_2O of unadulterated lust. We spoke nary a word to each other unless those words were "more," "stop messing with my hair," and "we need to change the drapes." The attraction was primal, carnal, pure animal. Like two rabid dogs humping the exhaust pipe of a Pinto, we set each other on fire.

Memories fade in and out of my mind's eye, but I do recall one moment, seen through the wispy gauze of sexual nostalgia. It was a Wednesday afternoon. Martha lay in bed, white linen sheets draped over half of her body. Her voice floated toward me like the sweet chirpings of a songbird: "You know this means nothing, right? This sex, it's just that, sex. There's nothing more, no future between us." I stood in the shadows of the bathroom, grasping the medicine cabinet, and my whole body shook. "Oh, this," I said with all the bravery I could muster. "Of course. You didn't even have to say that. I thought it was . . . I mean there could never be a future for us . . . right?" I had entered the bedroom by now, hoping to look into her eyes to see if she felt the same way I did. But she had turned her back to me. The sheet's gentle rise and descent told me she slept the sleep of the innocent, unaware of the pain she had inflicted. I sank into bed and wept. Martha left the next day.

We've seen each other since, in passing, at benefits, wine tastings, Shaquille O'Neal's birthday party. Cordial as always when we greet, pecks on the cheek, a dainty hug—to an outsider we resemble nothing more than civil business partners. Behind my genteel demeanor, though, lurks a wounded lion still in love. It's all I can do not to sweep aside the shrimp cocktail and tuna casserole from the catering table and possess her once again. Somehow I manage. Maybe my hand lingers too long and too fondly on hers when I say that my assistant will call hers on Monday morning, but if that is my greatest transgression, then I deserve no admonition. A final memory: our breakfast on that last morning in the South Pacific. Martha wrestled with her grapefruit, her Williams-Sonoma stainless steel spoon trying to pierce the skin of the bitter fruit. As she stabbed the fruit over and over she said, "Never mix business with pleasure. There are no real friendships in the business world, just stepping-stones to the next big thing. Invest in the stock market, not in another person."

She had done it. The grapefruit was conquered and she dove into the red pulpy mass with relish. A stream of tart juice pierced my eye. It stung.

CHAPTER 8

LET'S TEE IT UP AND GET THIS MEETING UNDER WAY: SPORTS IN OFFICESPEAK

Men, historically, have overrun the business world. And men, historically, have devotedly followed sports. This is not a coincidence. Most businessmen are failed athletes. As boys they dreamed of hitting the game-winning home run in the bottom of the ninth or catching the touchdown pass as time expired. As for myself, I spent many a midsummer eve dreaming of captaining the country club's equestrian team to a first place in dressage. In my scenario, the team had floundered and it all came down to me and my gallant steed Executive Decision to save the day. We succeeded beautifully, of course. I can still picture Executive Decision now, his mane braided and intertwined throughout with yellow ribbons, his black coat lustrous like vinyl, his eyes afire, his hooves immaculately mani-cured. I too looked exceptionally smart in my red riding jacket and white jodhpurs.

Flaubert wrote that somewhere in the moldy remains of a notary's heart lies a poet. The same could be said for the modern businessman, except we would have to change "notary" to "modern businessman" and "poet" to "jock." But once that's done, we've cap-tured the essence of the twenty-first-century office worker. The com-petitive fires that stoked him on the playground have been rekindled in the boardroom. That's why an office can resemble more of a locker room than a proper work environment once the testosterone levels reach their threshold. At heart, the men in your office are still little boys, still dreaming of sandlot glory. But the boardroom is their gridiron now, and every meeting is the Super Bowl. And so they rally the team and exhort their teammates with all the brio of football coaches. They couch their most profound thoughts in sports imagery because that's the only poetry they know; the poetry of Brent Musburger calling a game from the "big house" in Ann Arbor, Michigan, or the whisper of Jim Nantz from hallowed Augusta National. Is their behavior ridiculous and over-the-top at times? Yes. But let us men have our fun; it's all that's left us these days. Let us dream and be boys again.

Below are examples of commonly used sports terms that have been incorporated into everyday officespeak. Sports terms add a certain cachet to your conversation that says, "I'm above the law and will bend the rules as often as possible." Master them and you will be one of the boys, for better or worse.

Baseball

- "We've got to hit this one out of the park."
- "Kelly, I just want to touch base with you on the progress of your presentation."
- "Great going, Rob. You're batting a thousand after that meeting."
- "Sales have jumped right off the bat."

"Kelly, I'm gonna need you to pinch hit for me tomorrow at the meeting. Doris is pregnant again and she's dragging me to that sonogram thing they do. Just makes your kid look like an alien. I don't want to see it, but she's complaining again."

Football

"Jimmy, I need you to be the quarterback on the Reynolds account."

"The fourth-quarter results are in and they ain't good. We're gonna have to toss up a Hail Mary."

"Okay, everybody, let's huddle up and air out some ideas."

"No time for jokes, people, this is sudden death."

"We need to tackle this problem head-on."

Horse Racing

"It's coming down to the wire."

"Jerome is a dark horse to get the nod for the VP post."

"We gotta pick ourselves back up and get into the saddle again."

Basketball

"That presentation was a slam dunk."

"Nothing but net."

Tennis

"Game, set, match, we smoked the competition, boys."

Golf

⌐ "That's just par for the course."

⌐ "Let's tee it up and get started."

Fishing

⌐ "I want everyone to cast around with their different clients and see who bites."

Hockey

⌐ "We're in a face-off with Goldman Sachs over who gets the client."

And even more sports terms!

softball question	saddle up
curveball	fast track
three strikes rule	hurdles to overcome
time out	reel in a good catch
let's bounce some ideas around	hole in one
marathon project	hook, line, and sinker
race to the finish	fish for answers
blitz	below par

How do you set yourself apart amidst this deluge of sports idioms? As you know, the only way to get anywhere is to make yourself stand out. You need to prove to your boss that you are an innovative employee, someone who can contribute radical new ideas. And retreading the same old terms (a trend known as "Deja Moo") will give you all the authority of a benchwarmer. I've included below some exciting spins on sports we all know, as well as a list of more obscure activities and their corresponding idioms. It's bold, it's different, it's the Fosbury Flop. Use these terms and everyone in the office will want to sleep with you.

Football

☞ "Your ideas stink like a rotten jock strap."

Baseball

☞ "Don't just scratch your crotches, let's get back to work, everyone. Martha will be fine, epilepsy is not contagious."

☞ "If you don't have enough data, just inject some human growth hormone in the numbers. No one tests for it."

Basketball

☞ "Tom, if you land the McGivens account, then your next trip to the lap dancing parlor is on me."

Deep Sea Diving

☞ "Whoa, this meeting is giving me the bends."

Log Rolling

☞ "Put your back heel down first and keep spinning the log. We need to come up with more ideas."

Croquet

☞ "Great job, Kate, you knocked it through the wicket."

Figure Skating

☞ "I just read your report, Brad. You landed a triple salchow with this one, congratulations. I always knew you had it in you."

Competitive Hot Dog Eating

☞ "Squeeze the air out of the bun, then dip it in water, then break the hot dog into pieces and alternately eat the hot dog and bun, that's how you're going to meet your deadline."

NASCAR

☞ "If you want to get out of here before three in the morning, then you're gonna have to get two right-side tires and make a wedge adjustment on that sales report."

Miniature Golf

☞ "I like the way you think, Harry. Just put that idea through the windmill, bounce it off the clown's face, and see where it lands."

In the Trenches:
War and Officespeak

For some people, sports aren't enough. These people crave the confrontational, the aggressive, the violent. They scorn today's youth as being a bunch of hippie-dippie louts who could use a shave and a haircut. They walk around the office with corncob pipes wedged between their teeth, service revolvers hanging at their sides. When you go into their offices, you notice tapestry-size maps of the company's floor plan tacked up to the walls. Red and green arrows swarm around the blueprint and tiny army men and tanks seem to have set up camp right outside your cubicle. These people dreamed as children of riding with Genghis Khan, raping and pillaging across Central Asia. They are the warmongers in your office, and their language reflects this passion. Sure, they might be terrifying and irrational, but when the walls are crumbling about you, there's no one you'd rather have lead the charge to profitability.

War terminology should be used only when you need to make an important point. Save these big guns for those moments when you want everyone to stand at attention and listen to you. Here are some to get started with:

- "We're in the middle of a take-no-prisoners bidding war, team. Let's shock and awe the competition into an unconditional surrender."

☞ "By the time this meeting is through, there will be a high body count in this boardroom."

☞ "Man your posts, soldiers, it's gonna be a long night."

☞ "We've got to ambush our competitors."

☞ "That's on my radar screen."

☞ "Draw up a battle plan."

☞ "We shouldn't go into this meeting without some ammunition."

☞ "I'm gunning for that manager position."

☞ "I can't believe you went AWOL during the biggest conference of the year."

☞ "I don't want there to be a lot of fallout from this decision."

☞ "Eliminate the pockets of resistance now. Pick 'em off one by one if you have to. Show no mercy. I want my plan to be implemented."

☞ "Open the nerve gas canister and paralyze the competition."

Like a nuclear bomb, use these war terms sparingly, but to devastating effect. You will inspire fear and loyalty among your peers.

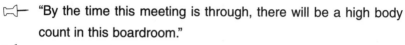

True Story: Cycling with Lance Armstrong

Yes, I had a car pulling me, but I still pedaled the entire way. Lance Armstrong and I were biking up the Andes on a route I had carved out myself some years before when I was bored and wished to see if those famed mountains could challenge me. They couldn't. I beat Lance to the top by a good three days. As I enjoyed a freshly chilled Yoo-hoo while overlooking the splendid ruins of Machu Picchu, I thought to myself, "Maybe he's not as spectacular as everybody has fooled themselves into believing." I don't want to get into a game of one-upmanship but I once survived a bout of adult chicken pox, no mean feat, and came back even stronger to lead my company's intramural handball team to the championship. The day of the final I had a temperature of 100.2. Maybe it's not nut cancer, but it ain't a stroll in the park either. But enough about my inner struggles and personal resolve, enough about the unquench-able flame that burns in my soul. As I sat on top of that mountain, I wanted to see what had become of this supposed superman.

I never should have doubted Lance. He has titanium in his blood. This man they call Armstrong has stainless steel in his bones. He apologized for being three days late and told me a rabid llama had delayed his ascent. This llama had terrorized a local village for years, and Lance took it upon himself to free the simple villagers from the savage grip of this merciless animal. Over the course of two days, he wrestled the monster to the ground, placed it in a choke hold, and then implacably looked on as he drained the life force from its body. His vanquishing of the beast was greeted with thunderous "Huzzahs" and plates of tamales and six virgin brides. Yes, I liked this man they called the Texan. As we sipped Mojitos that evening, I asked him how he had won six consecutive Tours de France. Lance smiled, took a bite of his cookie-dough-flavored PowerBar, and said, "I just put it into another gear, man. I put it into another gear." Figuratively and literally.

CHAPTER 9

I THINK YOU'RE NEAT, GIVE ME A RAISE: THE ART OF PERSUASION

Outside of your first DUI, there are few moments in life when you have to be more persuasive than when you are gunning for that raise or trying to hold on to your job. You need to appear calm, cool, and collected and able to recite the alphabet backward; one screwup and you're out on the street without a penny to your name. But it doesn't have to be like that. With just a few simple pointers you can be leading the high life all over again. The other time that you need to be as persuasive is when your wife discovers that you have a parallel life: another house, wife, and kids. That can be a real doozy to talk your way out of. Feel free to use some of the tips below in that situation as well.

SHOW ME THE MONEY: HOW TO GET THAT RAISE

You've earned it. Whether by being the good soldier and doing everything that's asked of you, or by bringing a fresh approach to a mundane job, you truly deserve a raise. Now you just need to muster the nerve to ask for one. No problem. Take a deep breath and do as I say. You can trust me.

Many of the techniques outlined in Chapter 7 recommended

befriending the players in your office; these same concepts can be recycled when dealing with your boss. About a month before you plan to ask for a raise, begin taking notes on phrases he utters and points he makes in meetings. When he's on the treadmill in the office gym, nonchalantly sidle up next to him and parrot back his statements. Compliment his clothes, and if your boss is a woman, ask if she's lost some weight, then cast a lingering glance along her figure. The process of buttering up your superiors should be timed so as not to raise suspicions that you are merely flattering them in order to get money. It should appear as though you are sincerely enamored with their business expertise. Never ever underestimate the blinders people wear when being flattered.

You've basted your boss in the grease of sycophancy, and now's the time to reap your reward. Dress well, but not too well. You don't want to enter the room with an air of premeditation, as though fate has ordained you to receive this bountiful raise. You want your boss to feel as though he has the final say in the matter. Exude an aura of confidence, believe for one sterling moment that, yes, you are indeed an essential employee.

When pleading your case, be sure to stop using the passive voice and make all of your statements active. Well, at least the ones where you have done something positive. Use strong, powerful verbs, not those weak, foppish ones. Here are some examples of verbs that will seize your boss's attention:

✐ "I *implemented* changes to our processing software that resulted in a fifteen percent increase in application efficiency."

⟋ "I *mediated* conflicts between clients and customers."

⟋ "I *fostered* a sense of camaraderie with my 'Stone the Weak Link in the Office' initiative."

Below are more verbs sure to make the management sit up and take notice of how much you do for the company.

pioneered	conceptualized	augmented
spearheaded	revolutionized	boosted
disseminated	collaborated	broadened
enforced	facilitated	revamped
apprised	arbitrated	utilized

It is also helpful to possess *leverage.* What makes you different from the rest, what's unique about you? Why do you deserve that raise? The following phrases will make your boss's knees buckle at the prospect of your leaving:

⟋ "Who's going to print out your e-mails if I'm gone?"

⟋ "There's a reason I never taught you how to use Excel. To make myself indispensable."

✐ "Who will cancel all of your appointments so you can play golf and then tell everyone you're at your daughter's piano recital?"

✐ "I'm the only person in the office who can put up with your shit."

✐ "You don't give me a raise, and I go public about your online handle: 'underagegothchick.'"

Follow these simple steps and you'll have so much money you might even consider donating some of it to charity. Until you see that sparkly new Rolex. The poor will always be there—treat yourself to some bling-bling.

CRAFT THE PERFECT MEMO TO SAVE YOUR JOB

You've heard the rumors, the whisperings in the halls. At lunch, in some clandestine corner of the cafeteria, a cabal of you and your colleagues have conferred about the warning signs: the muted e-mails from HR, your manager ominously stating that "some changes are going to have to be made." Yes, like a cat in heat, you can smell the layoffs that are about to come.

Once these initial murmurings begin to percolate, it behooves you to implement a plan of action. Unless you have a trust fund or a wealthy cancer-ridden uncle, you probably need to keep your job, and I will show you how. It's not difficult, and it just might save your life.

The first step is a subtle and effective campaign of misinformation. Once you know layoffs are imminent, begin convincing your colleagues that, in fact, no one will be fired. You are all vying for a limited number of spots, so the less competition you have, the better—especially considering that I doubt you are a model employee. That you are even reading this book instead of working on a PowerPoint presentation or researching market trends speaks volumes about your industriousness.

Sow the seeds of doubt in your coworkers' minds. Tell them that you talked to your friend in HR, and she vouched that no one was getting fired. The company is just cutting back on perks like petty cash and car service for the executives. Things that don't affect the hoi polloi. The weak will take the bait with this gambit, but the true sharks in the office will remain dubious. For them, you need to brew an irresistible bucket of chum.

I suggest forging a confidential memo, purportedly from the president of your company to the chief financial officer. I've always said, if you're going to forge, then forge big.

It should read something along these lines:

INTEROFFICE MEMORANDUM

From: Clifford Corcoran, President
To: Patrick Adams, CFO
RE: Second-quarter figures

Pat,

Troubling news looking over these second-quarter figures. The genie is out of the bottle; we're going to have to increase salaries across the board. I was hoping we could still operate on this shoestring budget of ours, but it looks like we've put ourselves on the map. Don't make waves with me on this one, Pat—I've drawn a line in the sand and I hope you'll join me on the winning side. I've had almost enough of your pooh-poohing. You can only pooh-pooh so much until the one being pooh-poohed can't handle being pooh-poohed anymore. So long story short, no more pooh-poohing from you. Let's set this organization on its ear and give something back to the employees. A rising tide lifts all boats. I look forward to your response. Oh, and let's keep a low profile on this one, maybe leak some bad intel about how jobs are on the bubble. That way, when everyone receives the good news, they will think of us as miracle workers and become even more indebted to us for their jobs. Just an idea on how to maintain loyalty. Let me know your thoughts.

Best,

Cliff

P.S. My compliments to your wife for her marshmallow ambrosia. Just delightful. [If the CFO is a woman, throw in a line about her husband's superior skills on the grill.]

Sure, the stuff about "pooh-poohing" might seem a tad juvenile, but no one knows what these people are really like. A touch of eccentricity lends credibility. Toss in a bunch of classic office terms such as "shoestring budget" and "keep a low profile" and you have yourself a masterpiece. Leave it in the copier just before one of your colleagues goes to use it.

Now it's your turn. You need to convince your boss that you are an indispensable cog in the office machinery.

INTEROFFICE MEMORANDUM

Dear Boss,

I wanted to complimentize you for the way you handled yourself at this morning's meeting. Very impressive. You took the bull by the horns and wrestled it to the ground. I agree, we need to refocus our efforts on streamlining the shipping and receiving department. It's time to knuckle down and step up to the plate regarding our inefficiencies.

And that's another topic I wanted to discuss with you. I want you to see me as an integral member of this team. Why, just the other day I was talking to [Client A] and they mentioned that I exemplified the can-do, gung-ho spirit that they associate with our company. They called me a true "go-getter." I don't want to toot my own horn or anything, but I thought I'd bring it to your attention. Clients like me, they really like me.

I also thought you should know about the diminished performance of John and Katie. They are both wonderful people, but wonderful people don't always make great workers. I don't want to be a snitch, but they spend a lot of time e-mailing friends, making dinner reservations on the phone, and organizing happy hour activities. Again, I love them as people, I'm just very concerned that their actions are adversely affecting the bottom line. They don't strike me as team players.

In closing, when office personnel get streamlined in the upcoming weeks, I trust you will think of me as a vital member of this organization. I see myself as the pancreas of the company: often overlooked, sometimes misunderstood, but vital to the company's survival. We don't have a lot of face time together, so I just wanted to touch base with you on this topic. Oh, and remember, I have photos of your escapades in Reno during the sales conference.

Best,

D. W.

This is an excellent letter that I have used on numerous occasions. Rat out your colleagues whenever you have the opportunity to do so—remember, they'd do the same to you. And in my vast experience I have found that having dirt on your boss or any other higher-up can only help your cause.

Hot Tip: Make Your Own Business Card

Nothing says "class" like your own business card, especially if you're not important enough to merit one at your job. The business card is your opportunity to present yourself to the world through graphics. If you're a stockbroker, put some clip art of the scrolling Dow Jones on your card. If you're an attorney, why not toss in a drawing of one of those wigs the British lawyers wear, and if you're a consultant, have a drawing of a guy shoveling manure in the upper right-hand corner. (I'm only teasing, although I do know a consultant who has a card with this drawing, and it's a wonderful conversation piece.) These are simple ways to spruce up your card and to make yourself stand out from the crowd. If you have the money to splurge on a hologram business card, by all means do so.

This is also a great time to enhance your job title. No one ever fact-checks a business card. People believe what they read. If your card says "President of AT&T," then the receiver of your card will think that you are the president of AT&T. Now, I do not advocate such radical self-promotion as this, but I see nothing wrong with adding an Executive here, or a Senior Manager there. There's a surfeit of VPs, Assoc. VPs, Execs, Sr. Execs, and Jr. Managers; nobody can keep track of what they mean anymore, if indeed they still mean anything. So join the fray and tack on one of these titles; you'll feel much more important. No one pushes around a Senior Executive Associate Vice President of Sales, do they?

WORK AMPLIFICATION: HOW TO ACT AND SOUND MORE IMPORTANT THAN YOU REALLY ARE TO FRIENDS AND FAMILY

Sometimes the hardest people to impress aren't your colleagues but your family. They expect greatness from you, and nothing less will satisfy their insatiable appetite to brag about you to the neighbors. In their eyes you are the golden child, or at least their ticket to an early retirement. But you know the truth, you're stuck in the usual office job, the usual rut, crunching numbers, making copies, surfing the Internet, waiting for something better to come along, wondering if all that schooling you went through wasn't just a complete waste of time. Your friends and family don't have to know this, though, and it's better if they don't. You want to be a somebody around them, and I have just the pointers for you to pull off this charade.

Appearance is everything. The first Christmas after my twenty-third birthday I pulled into my parents' driveway in a vintage 1963 Maserati with a bottle of 1948 Krug in tow. I possessed all the trappings of success, from my hand-stitched Testoni shoes to an original copy of the Declaration of Independence that my manservant Tumba carted around on his back at all times—it was evident that I had made it. You, of course, unless you possess an unlimited bank account, will find it difficult to replicate such a stunning debut. But here are some ideas:

Rent an Italian sports car. No one has to know it's not yours. Also, rent hot women to fill up the backseat of the Italian sports car. No one has to know they're hookers.

 Stress that, like a doctor, you are always on call. Prearrange with a friend at work to have him call your cell phone three or four times during dinner with the family (a technique you may remember from Chapter 3). When the phone rings, smile, shrug your shoulders, and say, "It's like this all the time. Sometimes I wish I weren't so good." For bonus points have your phone go off in the middle of the night.

 Employ newspaper snobbery. Complain about the lack of the *Wall Street Journal* and the business section of the *New York Times* lying around the house. "How am I supposed to keep up with the markets? This is my job we're talking about!" Drop the word "markets" frequently throughout conversations and stress how you always need to be updated about their status. Don't worry if your job has absolutely nothing to do with the stock market; that you even know to bandy about the term "markets" will demonstrate that you are a major player, whatever your industry may be.

 Make references to the Fed. On a similar note, if you feel that the "markets" gambit is going over well, go in for the kill and mention that you "can't believe what the Fed is doing to the interest rates." No one really understands what the Fed does or why interest rates are important—so be the person who does know.

 Curse. A lot. People who curse are important—it's that simple. They have so much stress in their lives, such incredible responsibility, that the part of their brain that controls vocabulary has to siphon off energy to other parts of the brain, thus leaving them with only a few crude terms at their disposal. If you ask me, "sonofabitch," exclaimed in a drawn-out, high-pitched whine is the signature call of the king of the business jungle.

Below, I have demonstrated a few of the myriad ways in which to pepper your everyday speech with words like "son-of-a-bitch" (and other notable curse words):

- "Sonofabitch, Bill. You told me the numbers would be ready by today. Not to-fuckin'-morrow but today. Dipshit."
- "Dammit, Mom, the potatoes are cold. Sonofabitch."
- "Where the hell is the goddamned paper, Dad? Sonofabitch."
- "Shit, Grandma, did you see the interest rates? Sonofabitch."

If you talk like this, not only will you intimidate all of your loved ones into not prying further into your desultory career, but you will exude all the alpha traits of a true power broker. It's okay to be an asshole, especially when you want to impress friends and family.

Watch CNBC. Turn on CNBC, scream "dammit," toss the remote at the screen, and storm out of the room. Return fifteen minutes later, interrupt whatever program your family is watching, turn the channel back to CNBC, and mutter, "Jesus Christ, this is why I don't go on vacation."

One-upmanship. When talking with friends about each other's jobs and careers, master the subtle art of one-upmanship. If one of your buddies gets a raise, mention how two companies are in a "high-stakes bidding war" for your services. If another boasts the use of a company car, show them the limo company you have on speed dial.

Treat your mother like the secretary you claim to have. Leave memos around the house ordering her to clean the bathroom, dust the bookcases, and for God's sake do something about the tacky Christmas decorations. Inform her that you plan to follow through with her about her progress shortly. "There will be ramifications." See how she likes having the tables turned.

Throw out your wallet and get a money clip. Wallets are for those who need to be encumbered with credit cards, photo IDs, and family pictures. Money clips say, "My Benjamins kiss sterling silver as I tuck them into bed." And they also say, "Excuse me, but I can pay my way out of any situation I find myself in." When you go out for dinner, even if (God forbid) it's Applebee's or Bennigan's, palm twenties to the hostess and your server. Even tip your dad for driving everyone out to the restaurant. Gratuitous disregard for money is the cornerstone of the successful.

 Fake or honestly acquire a cocaine addiction. Yes, it's eighties retro, but it's also timeless. Leave orange-tinted pill bottles, speckled with a dash of flour (or coke, again, if you really have a habit), scattered around the house, constantly tweak and rub your nose, and alternate between moods of euphoria and moods of despair bordering on paranoia. If you have a backyard pool, I highly recommend sitting in a lawn chair on the diving board wearing your high school varsity jacket and a pair of shades. Kitschy, yes, but it is the tableau for the successful and the dissolute.

Not everything in life goes according to plan, however. I should know, my three children were born after my vasectomy. So let's crack open another can of beluga caviar and delve into the language of getting fired.

CHAPTER 10

CONGRATULATIONS, YOU'VE JUST RECEIVED AN INVOLUNTARY RELEASE FROM YOUR WORKSTATION

He was forty-three and had a wife and three kids. One of his children was supposedly brilliant, had an IQ of 160, read Shakespeare's complete works by his fifth birthday. The public schools in his area teach kids how to survive a knife fight and how to deliver a baby in the bathroom stall. So the only option was this private school with a tuition of $40,000 a year, a hefty price regardless, but even heftier considering he had just gotten into a massive car accident that totaled his vehicle and had left the other driver in the hospital. He was going to have to take on some of those costs, and his insurance company would drop him shortly thereafter. This prologue presents a worst-case scenario (and this one is true) of somebody who desperately needed his job and literally could not afford to lose it.

I fired him. The stress of his personal life clung to him like a vine, eventually smothering his capacity to function in the office. I'd like to think I cushioned the blow with a few choice words and a poem I had composed. I've always prided myself on my people skills, my ability to relate to the "others" in the work environment, those dispensable to the company's mission. Whether it's a pat on the head or a lollipop after the completion of a big assignment, I tend to go that extra mile when caring for my employees. And when it comes to the oftentimes irksome business of firing someone, I have developed the perfect language for delivering what is to some a deathblow. Yes, that man wept like a schoolgirl witnessing her prized copy of *Tiger Beat* torn to shreds by unruly boys. And yes, the security guards had to carry him out of the office as he cried over and over, "Why me? Why me?" But like a two-legged cat, he eventually landed on his feet. About a year ago I came across his name in the police blotter section of the local paper. He and a high school girl had been found in a compromising position across the hood of his 1987 Datsun (I guess he had to sell his BMW), which is a big no-no. But the silver lining here is that she worked for him at the Hollywood Video store he managed; I always knew he had the gifts to become a persuasive manager. And now he's managing the Rockford Penitentiary basketball team. Everything works out for the best; life's a funny journey.

This section is for the managers out there, for the people who have responsibility over other people, for the people who control the destiny of others. I hope this chapter will allow you to discover some merciful ways to let those loyal to you know that they need to leave their desk by noon or else they will be forcibly removed from the premises.

SEE ME

Two words: "see" and "me." Every worker knows that nothing of any good can follow this command. It's the workplace equivalent of a girl telling you that she just wants to be friends. Only doom and heartbreak remain.

That being said, I recommend that you begin any layoff process with those two words. It's better not to mislead the employee or get his or her hopes up by saying something like, "I've got great news, Rich. I'm going to give you the opportunity to sleep in every morning and take that cross-country road trip you're always babbling about." Once you see the stupefied grin unfold across his or her face, it does, admittedly, become a tad difficult to say, "Because you're fired." In my experience using this approach, an office chair is bound to leave its allotted spot on the floor and find itself crashing through the window.

When you fire someone, remember to put all the emphasis on the person being fired. Try to stay in the background as much as possible. Use "you" sentences, not "I" ones. That way, later, when the person recalls getting fired, it will be more difficult for him or her to remember who did it. Also, don't use the person's name. Names only personalize everything and drive home the point that the employee is indeed getting fired. And, if possible, couch the firing in terms that make it seem as if this decision is in the best interest of the firee. At its best the language of firing can eerily resemble the language of breaking up:

- "You've been a great employee for the past five years, but it's time you moved on."
- "Don't you think you've become a little bored here? Someone as smart and creative as you are needs to be challenged. Do yourself a favor and find another job."
- "It's not you. It's the company. You're perfect, don't change."

☞ "You're going to be missed. You know that, right? The office won't be the same without you."

☞ "You are a special person. In fact, you're more special as a person than as an employee, and that's why you have to leave."

☞ "Never turn off that special light that makes you uniquely you. Now back up and exit the building. Now."

☞ "Hey, keep in touch. Don't be a stranger, you hear?"

☞ "Have you looked at yourself recently? You're a mess. You need time off, time to sort yourself out. This is best for you. See the wife and kids. Oh, that's right, I forgot, Judy has full-time custody. Well, at least you get to work on your putting, right? And that ain't a bad thing!"

☞ "Let's still be friends."

Many times the employee getting fired will become anxious and confrontational when hearing the news. He or she will probably blame you for the firing and ask for the rationale. Unless the employee has committed a specific transgression leading to the firing (such as stealing from the company, laziness, trying to take your job), the reasons for his or her being fired are probably multitudinous. Or maybe the company is just trying to cut costs. Or the employee has outlived his or her usefulness. Either way, you don't want to completely gut the person, so always emphasize how hard you fought for him or her but that inevitably the vast, faceless entity known as "they" or "them" had the final say. Leave it unspoken that you yourself are just at the mercy of "them." Of course, these are all lies, but they are good lies:

- ☞ "I would love to help you, but my hands are tied."
- ☞ "Your guess is as good as mine. Sometimes they make crazy decisions."
- ☞ "Listen, this isn't my decision. You know that if it were up to me I'd keep you. But it's not up to me, it's up to them."
- ☞ "This came from the muckety-mucks above. They never consult me on this type of stuff."
- ☞ "What can I say? I fought for you, Bob. Tooth and nail—I did. But they had already made up their minds."
- ☞ "Weird things are going on in this company. To be honest, I think this is a blessing in disguise."
- ☞ "I probably shouldn't even be telling you this, but since I like you, here it is: They're restructuring the whole infrastructure of the company. I envy you, actually. Any one of us could go at any time."
- ☞ "Don't think of this as a firing. Think of it as a graduation from the workplace. I do believe some congratulations are in order!"

Sometimes, though, you revel in the employee getting fired. Maybe it's a snot-nosed brat who got too big for his britches or a gadfly who was always questioning your decisions and talking behind your back. These are the moments that managers live for, when you can use your authority and turn the screw a notch on your office enemies. You can make up any outlandish reason you like for crushing these minions. You're never going to see these people again. Have fun.

- ✄ "I looked over your résumé one more time and saw that you majored in Mishandling Funds while at Harvard. You've done them proud."
- ✄ "This isn't personal, but the sight of your smile each morning makes me want to disembowel myself and then consume my own intestines. Kind of ironic, no?"
- ✄ "This is a Mets office, Yankees suck, now get out." (Can be used for all sports teams.)
- ✄ "Don't think we don't notice the rampant theft of three-ring binders. We're not morons, you know!"
- ✄ "No one wants to hear about your newborn baby anymore. Everyone has one, it's not that interesting."
- ✄ "We have you on videotape touching yourself while looking at the J.Crew catalog online. There's just no place for a sick pervert like you at our company."

INVOLUNTARY RELEASE
FROM WORKSTATION

So far we've dealt with the more personal side of firing someone. The language has been gentle, sympathetic, reassuring even. This nurturing officespeak is used for someone you know personally, somebody you maybe even like, someone who deserves a loving hand when being told that he or she is just a piece of corporate driftwood. It's like the soft cooing sounds you make before you put down a beloved pet.

But the majority of layoffs you will oversee will be of the large, impersonal kind. A tightening of the budget strings and a dozen or so unnecessary folk must go. And if your company finds itself in dire straits, then the numbers go up. The best way to handle necessary layoffs is through a jargon-heavy vocabulary. Never use the term "layoffs" or even "downsizing"—most everybody has wised up to that one by now. Instead, force yourself to stretch your creative muscle and discover new ways of camouflaging the word "fired." You know you've crafted the perfect statement if no one is quite certain what you mean. Obfuscate, obfuscate, obfuscate. When it comes to announcing unpopular news, be as unclear as possible. Also, this is a perfect opportunity to put your passive voice skills to the test. Remember, passive voice negates accountability. No one is to blame when the passive voice is used—that's one of its many beauties.

These are my own sentences. I've used each of these at one time or another to lay off anywhere between five thousand and fifty thousand employees, and I've always received an overwhelmingly positive response. Feel free to make them your own:

✐ "Due to a paradigm shift in the corporate goal-setting for the 2006 fiscal year, a mandate has been executed requiring a dismissal of surplus tasking."

- "Management concerns over share value necessitates that a reconfiguring of the office personnel be implemented." (Notice the exquisite use of passive voice in "be implemented." It does not mention who will implement this layoff—all hands have been washed clean. And for what it's worth, "reconfiguring" is the new "downsizing"—a personal favorite of mine.
- "At this juncture, it has been deemed prudent to offer employees voluntary separation incentives." (Think of being fired as a gift given by the company.)
- Effective immediately, our fiscal strategy requires a loosening of all skilled workers."

I WANT TO SPEND MORE TIME WITH MY FAMILY: HOW TO SAVE FACE WHEN YOU BECOME EXPENDABLE

How many times have you read in the paper that some high-powered executive is leaving his seven-figure job because he wants to spend more time with the wife and kids? Too many. Trust me, I work with these people—I *am* one of these people, and we'd rather have a hot poker speared through our eyeball than attend Timmy's soccer game or snuggle in with the wife on a Sunday morning. Do you think any family is worth a seven-figure salary? No, of course not. There's a reason we entered the high-stakes world of corporate life: so we'd have an excuse not to be with our families. But it makes us sound like good people, your average Joe, just longing to escape the confines of the office and be encased in the warm fuzziness of home.

Everybody gets fired sometime, and the following phrases will help you save face amongst your peers and family. Or at the very least, you'll convince yourself that you're saving face.

- "The company and I have agreed to go in different directions."
- "We had artistic differences."
- "I just felt that it was time for a change of scenery."
- "I accomplished everything I set out to do, and now I'm off to discover new challenges."
- "I have the utmost respect for the CEO. We just didn't see eye-to-eye on the direction for the company."
- "I've always wanted to direct, actually."
- "My two-, no, three-year-old daughter called me 'stranger man' last night, so I think I should spend more time at home so that little brat knows to call me 'sir.'"
- "There's this continuing ed class in pottery I was really hoping to take, but it conflicted with all the late nights I spent at the office."
- "I always promised my folks I would get that PhD in art history some day."
- "It was such a long commute, you know, I'm looking for something closer to home."
- "I figure I shop at the Gap all the time, why not get that employee discount?"

True Story: Subway Surfing with Donald Trump

I don't want to take credit for Donald Trump's catchphrase "You're fired" (after all, it's not as if he invented the line), but after a particularly exhilarating late night of subway surfing, I did strongly suggest that he deliver the salvo with a snakelike projection of the hand. God is in the details. Unfortunately, God doesn't get paid royalties for such suggestions. Or receive thank-you notes.

CHAPTER 11

I'LL HAVE YOU CLONED:
BUSINESS TALK OF THE FUTURE

I know that the skeptics out there will dismiss this chapter as pure folderol. Who can predict the future? And if you could, why aren't you laying a cool thousand on the next Kentucky Derby champion or winning the Oscar office pool every year? My response to that is: The gift of prognostication must not be taken lightly. Those of us blessed with "the shining" should use our power not for personal gain but instead for the betterment of mankind.

After I spent a weekend binging on peyote in the badlands of South Dakota, the following phrases were revealed to me in a hallucinogenic haze. And for those skeptics out there, place $500 on Invincible Majesty to win in next year's Derby, and $500 on Matthew Lillard for best actor.

"I'll Have You Cloned!"

By the year 2020 cloning will not only be accepted but will be as mundane an activity as donating organs for androids. Multinational corporations will invest heavily in isolating the genes that promote "positive worker attributes." Once these genes have been identified, corporations will build cloning farms on which they harvest the perfect office worker. I have seen the perfect office worker. His name is Ted. He is 6'1", 180 pounds, with thinning brown hair and a winning smile—an indefatigable employee. He also rows and plays squash in his free time and hopes to travel across the United States when he retires. Ted is happily married, although on occasion he will stare longingly at a female employee. All of these components have been carefully selected for Ted in order to make him the most efficient and loyal employee. Tragically, Ted does not realize that when he turns sixty-five (the official retirement age), the company will "put him down." Corporations own the "life rights" to all cloned employees and will occasionally execute one at a boardroom meeting to insure against complacency from the "NCHs" (noncloned humans).

"But Will It Sell on Mars?"

This question will take Earth by storm after lone world superpower Newfoundland successfully colonizes Mars and builds the first strip mall on the red planet. Every product must pass the "Mars test"—a byword for universal appeal—before it gets the green light.

"It's a Suburb Out There."

The year 2050 marks the last gasp of the world's rainforests and jungles. It is believed that a jungle still exists somewhere in northwest

Cambodia, sandwiched between a Newfoundland Fried Chicken and a Virtual Pizza Hut, but this has not been confirmed. Regardless, nobody has seen a jungle in a decade and the phrase "It's a jungle out there" provides only bafflement. It is decided that the suburbs, with their parks and tree-lined avenues, most closely resemble the jungles of yore.

"Are You Plugged into This Discussion?"

Literally. All employees will have implanted (free of charge by MicrosoftDellGirlsGoneWild Incorporated) a dial-up connection at the base of the spine. This connection will allow them to send and receive e-mails via their brains as well as call up spreadsheets, PowerPoint presentations, and Doom 3000.

"Let's Throw a Googly at Them."

In a stunning reversal of fortune, cricket overtakes soccer as the world's most popular sport. Even the United States finds itself swept up into cricket fever when President Heath Ledger reveals his infatuation with the game as a tyke growing up in Australia. Americans everywhere shave their baseball bats in half and spend countless hours in the back-yard attempting to hit the deceptive googly. All officespeak sports idioms now contain only references to cricket.

"Robbing Ringo to Pay Paul."

A focus group survey reveals that ninety percent of MBAs do not realize that Peter and Paul were disciples of Christ. They just assumed they were roommates or cubemates. So in order to clarify the meaning, the Department of Speech Control changes the idiom to refer to two of the more lovable Beatles.

I have provided but a few of the various new terms coming soon to an office near you. Wow your colleagues, impress management, and earn the respect of the clairvoyant secretary by using these phrases decades before anyone else.

CONCLUSION

It is over. I have nothing left to teach you. Like a mother bird I have regurgitated the food of my business acumen and placed this gooey concoction upon your trembling tongue. You have been nourished by my wisdom. You have grown stout; your feathers are in fine plumage. It is time for you to go.

I beseech you to leave the nest, to spread your wings and conquer new worlds, to stab colleagues in the back, to pilfer employee retirement funds, to madden and confuse those around you with your mastery of officespeak. Cast aside the weak and the forlorn, embrace the strong and the merciless.

"And you?" I hear you asking. I'll be just fine. The autumn of my career approaches. It's a young person's world now, no place for an old codger like myself. Leave me here. Leave me to count my money. Don't worry about calling. Or stopping by on a rainy afternoon. I'll make do. It's lonely at the top.

Now go out and get 'em, champ! ;)